"Often, God does some of His deepest work in our lives through questions. That's why we find His questions throughout the Bible. In this book, Dr. Alemu Beeftu examines 31 of the questions God asked those He raised up as spiritual leaders. Their response to these questions shaped their lives and ministries.

"As you read this book, I pray God will work through these questions to bring you to a new place in your walk with Him as well! Allow Him to prepare you to be a more effective leader as you seek the answers to each question He poses to you in this book and in your intimate conversations with the King of kings and Lord of lords."

Dr. Robert D. Heidler, apostolic teacher,
Glory of Zion International Ministries

"In *Divine Dialogue*, my good friend Alemu Beeftu helps us explore 31 questions throughout Scripture, carefully studying the implications of each. Knowing that God does not ask questions out of His own curiosity, we are challenged then to move deeper into theological study, examining our own motives, response, and relationship with Him. I highly recommend this book if you are serious about becoming the kind of leader God desires."

Dr. Wess Stafford, president emeritus, Compassion International;
author, *Too Small to Ignore* and *Just a Minute*

"Most often when God encountered a leader with a question, He invited that leader to reflect on a deeper issue, which ended up in a significantly growing knowledge of God and deeper intimacy with Him. Alemu Beeftu writes from his own experience and through the unique way God has revealed His words to him. I highly recommend this book for those who want to explore the effectiveness of reflective leadership."

Bambang Budijanto, PhD, general secretary,
Asia Evangelical Alliance

"Why would an omnipotent God ask us questions when He obviously knows the answers? In *Divine Dialogue,* Alemu has selected 31 questions God asks in the Scriptures to challenge leaders to seek God for the right answers. God tells us that if any man lacks wisdom, we can ask Him. But how many of us really depend on Him for the answers, or do we merely trust our own experience? As I read this insightful book, I reflected on areas where I need to learn to ask God for the correct answers."

Larry E. Yonker, former president/CEO (retired),
Springs Rescue Mission

"Do you want to know God's heart, His divine will for you on your journey with Him? Then pay attention to the questions He asks along the way. My dear friend Alemu Beeftu unpacks a number of questions from Scripture and models for us how God does indeed ask questions of us that, if reflected on, will take us to a deeper level of understanding. *Divine Dialogue*, one of Alemu's finest that I've read, is like a road map for those of us who desire to draw deeply from Scripture and live out our calling with great joy. I highly recommend it."

Mark Yeadon, former senior vice president of
global program, Compassion International

DIVINE
DIALOGUE

Books by Alemu Beeftu and Chuck D. Pierce

Abiding in His Presence
The King's Signet Ring
Rekindle the Altar Fire

DIVINE DIALOGUE

ANSWER 31
GOD QUESTIONS
TO DISCOVER
HIS HEART
AND PURPOSE

Alemu Beeftu

Chosen
a division of Baker Publishing Group
Minneapolis, Minnesota

© 2025 by Alemu Beeftu

Published by Chosen Books
Minneapolis, Minnesota
ChosenBooks.com

Chosen Books is a division of
Baker Publishing Group, Grand Rapids, Michigan

Printed in the United States of America

All rights reserved. No part of this publication may be reproduced, stored in a retrieval system, or transmitted in any form or by any means—for example, electronic, photocopy, recording—without the prior written permission of the publisher. The only exception is brief quotations in printed reviews.

Library of Congress Cataloging-in-Publication Data
Names: Beeftu, Alemu author
Title: Divine dialogue : answer 31 God questions to discover his heart and purpose / Alemu Beeftu.
Description: Minneapolis, Minnesota : Chosen Books, a division of Baker Publishing Group, [2025]
Identifiers: LCCN 2024038812 | ISBN 9780800773236 (paperback) | ISBN 9780800773281 (casebound) | ISBN 9781493450947 (ebook)
Subjects: LCSH: Christian life—Biblical teaching | Bible—Criticism, interpretation, etc. | Devotional calendars
Classification: LCC BS680.C47 B43 2025 | DDC 248.4—dc23/eng/20250106
LC record available at https://lccn.loc.gov/2024038812

Unless otherwise indicated, Scriptures taken from the Holy Bible, New International Version®, NIV®. Copyright © 1973, 1978, 1984, 2011 by Biblica, Inc.® Used by permission of Zondervan. All rights reserved worldwide. www.zondervan.com. The "NIV" and "New International Version" are trademarks registered in the United States Patent and Trademark Office by Biblica, Inc.®

Scripture quotations identified ASV are from the American Standard Version of the Bible.

Scripture identified AMPC taken from the Amplified® Bible, Copyright © 1954, 1958, 1962, 1964, 1965, 1987 by The Lockman Foundation. Used by permission. lockman.org

Scripture quotations identified ESV are from The Holy Bible, English Standard Version® (ESV®), copyright © 2001 by Crossway, a publishing ministry of Good News Publishers. Used by permission. All rights reserved. ESV Text Edition: 2016

Scripture quotations identified GNT are from the Good News Translation in Today's English Version– Second Edition. Copyright © 1992 by American Bible Society. Used by permission.

Scripture quotations identified NASB taken from the (NASB®) New American Standard Bible®, Copyright © 1960, 1971, 1977, 1995 by The Lockman Foundation. Used by permission. All rights reserved. www.lockman.org

Scripture quotations identified MSG are taken from *The Message*, copyright © 1993, 2002, 2018 by Eugene H. Peterson. Used by permission of NavPress. All rights reserved. Represented by Tyndale House Publishers.

Scripture identified NCV taken from the New Century Version®. Copyright © 2005 by Thomas Nelson. Used by permission. All rights reserved.

Scripture identified NKJV taken from the New King James Version®. Copyright © 1982 by Thomas Nelson. Used by permission. All rights reserved.

Scripture quotations identified NLT are taken from the *Holy Bible*, New Living Translation, copyright © 1996, 2004, 2015 by Tyndale House Foundation. Used by permission of Tyndale House Publishers, Carol Stream, Illinois 60188. All rights reserved.

Cover design by InsideOut Creative Arts, Inc.

Baker Publishing Group publications use paper produced from sustainable forestry practices and postconsumer waste whenever possible.

25 26 27 28 29 30 31   7 6 5 4 3 2 1

This book is dedicated to my wife, Genet Y Beeftu. I am the most blessed person to have her as both the love of my life and a covenant friend. I have learned so much from her about how to have a true and honest dialogue with God in holy fear, with sincere faith, and with a pure conscience. I have also learned how to dialogue with others with a loving heart to highlight the truth that will set them free.

With a grateful heart and unspeakable joy, I also would like to recognize my children, Keah and Ammanuel, for giving me total freedom to dialogue with my heavenly Father, to hear His heart, and to obey His will as they were growing up.

CONTENTS

Foreword by Chuck D. Pierce   11
Introduction   15

PART ONE ◆ QUESTIONS OF DIVINE DIALOGUE   19

1. Will You Give Me a Drink?   21
2. Why Do You Cry?   27
3. Why Do You Persecute Me?   33
4. Where Are You?   39
5. Where Is Your Spouse?   45
6. Where Is Your Brother?   51
7. What Is Your Name?   57
8. Who Are You?   63
9. Who Do You Say I Am?   69
10. Do You Believe That I Am Able to Do This?   75

PART TWO ◆ QUESTIONS OF MIRACLES   81

11. Who Touched My Clothes?   83
12. What Do You Want Me to Do for You?   89
13. Friends, Haven't You Any Fish?   95
14. What Shall I Give You?   101

PART THREE ◆ QUESTIONS OF CHARACTER   107

15. Where Are My Honor and Reverence?   109
16. Where Are You Going?   115
17. What Is This Sound I Hear?   121
18. Who Are These Men with You?   127
19. Whose Portrait Is This?   133
20. Can These Bones Live?   139
21. What Is in Your Hand?   145
22. Who Is This Who Questions My Wisdom?   151

PART FOUR ◆ QUESTIONS OF VISION   157

23. What Do You See?   159
24. Whom Shall I Send?   165
25. Am I Not the One Who Is Sending You?   171
26. What Are You Doing in the Cave?   177
27. How Long Will You Mourn for Saul?   183

PART FIVE ◆ QUESTIONS OF AUTHORITY   189

28. Why Do You Cry to Me?   191
29. Why Have You Fallen on Your Face?   197
30. Why Are You Standing Here?   203
31. Do You Love Me More Than These?   209

Process the Questions   215
Conclusion   219
Acknowledgments   221

FOREWORD

Divine Dialogue is an incredible book that revolves around the concept of critical thinking. We have an image of what critical thinkers look like: masterminds sitting around a table, brooding over the piles of data strewn everywhere, when—*voilà!*—a "critical thought" arrives in the form of an answer to all the world's problems. Not so. The heart of critical thinking is not in the derived conclusions but in the process of asking questions—which is one way the Lord causes us to think differently. I love people who ask questions!

When we examine the teachings and ministry of Jesus, isn't it interesting that He, having all knowledge as the Son of God, chose to ask questions rather than just supply all the answers? The Lord asks us questions to cause us to think differently and critically. He stirs our minds and prompts us so that we will seek His way. I believe the Body of Christ is currently being prompted by grace to answer the Lord in a new way. Our hearts and minds are being stirred to ask a question similar to what is echoed throughout both Haggai 1 and Matthew 16—"What time is it in your life?" Do we truly understand the season we are presently in? This is a season when we should be responding to the Lord to gain triumph and victory, and the main question we have to answer is "Who do you say I am?" Every day, we need to respond to that question.

Have you ever noticed the questions that were asked of people throughout the Word of God? Every question demanded a response. We can surmise that for each question God, His Son, or His Spirit asks, we need to have a reply. God is sovereign, but He looks for our response. This is what makes our relationship with God so real. The Lord has never ceased interacting with His people. What He desires is a people willing to gather *His* thoughts, assess *His* ways, align with *His* strategies, and then move with a faith action. *Divine Dialogue* will help you align with God's thoughts. Here are a few keys to sharpen your mind and develop critical-thinking skills:

1. Define your problem and clarify your real concern.
2. Evaluate all information you have and then pinpoint the missing pieces so that you can develop complete thought processes.
3. Define your traps and biases.
4. Clarify your position and authority.
5. Identify root causes of the problem you are addressing.
6. Determine what point of view you are using in your analysis.
7. Be willing to shift your perspective at any time.
8. Ask yourself, "Am I limiting my thought processes to only what I know?" Limited thought processes are synonymous with self-righteousness.
9. Identify anything you are taking for granted in your analysis. Do not allow your assumptions to cause you to look foolish.
10. Check to make sure you are not making intellectual judgments based upon partial truths.

11. Ask yourself, "Have I simplified things to the point that I'm missing out on the major component here?"
12. Avoid being biased or prejudiced in the way you receive, perceive, and release information.

I think one of the most important questions God asks us is "Do you know how to receive grace?" Grace is acknowledging His kindness and goodness in the midst of life. We can't work for grace—nothing we can do produces the answer to grace. However, we can learn the ways of God and respond and receive it. Much of what is written here will cause you to understand grace.

I believe there are steps each of us can take to get to the moment in our life when God can extend grace. The Lord started His relationship with man once man deviated from his path by asking Adam, "Where are you?" Adam attempted to explain to God why he'd deviated and why he and the woman recognized they were naked, and God asked them another question: "Who told you that you were naked?" Then He asked a third question: "Have you eaten from the tree that I commanded you not to eat from?" Man had to respond with an answer.

Alemu helps you discover God's heart and purpose in your life through questions He will ask you as you walk with Him. You'll develop character, miracles, vision, authority, and relationships through the questions you and the Lord will share throughout your life.

Every key relationship has dialogue. I find that while we are a praying people, prayer has to be a dialogue in which you are listening for God to question what you are praying. *Divine Dialogue* is going to be a useful tool in helping you think critically before the Lord and answer questions—not only those you might have but questions He is asking you. This is a wonderful read!

Dr. Chuck D. Pierce, pesident, Glory of Zion International,
Kingdom Harvest Alliance

INTRODUCTION

We all ask questions. From the time you were old enough to speak, I bet you asked a lot of questions as you learned about the world around you. As an adult, you may ask a question to satisfy your personal curiosity or to confirm facts. You may ask a question to test someone else's understanding or learn something new. What about, however, when God asks a question?

Our sovereign God does not ask questions because He needs us to confirm facts. God asks questions to confirm and clarify something for the sake of His people. God's desire is that we recognize our state of being and come to grips with the situations in which we find ourselves. He also wants to reveal a deeper level of who He is. His questions expose deeper motives for repentance and restoration, facilitate change, and bring revelation. And the good news is that God did not relegate His inquiries to biblical times. He asks His questions today!

I have a good friend whose ministry efforts—after many years of hard work and steadfast obedience to God—were finally beginning to bear fruit and pay the bills. In the midst of this prosperous season, he sensed God calling him to shift the direction of the ministry. To do so would mean starting over from scratch. Needless to say, my friend had a difficult time believing that beginning anew was actually God's will for the organization. He asked himself, *Am I hearing God clearly in this?*

One night in prayer, he approached God. In all sincerity he asked, "But Father, what about my reputation?" The question had barely left his lips when he heard God answer the question thus: *What reputation?* My very wise friend subsequently changed his course in response to God's question.

Throughout Scripture, you will see many examples of God asking His people questions: Job, Micah, Moses, and so on. God still does this today, and understanding why He questions us is vital for us to be effective in our personal lives and in fulfilling our leadership roles. If you respond to God's questions in humility and from a place of brokenness, you will experience renewal, restoration, revival, victory, hope, healing, and a greater confidence in your relationship with Him.

God's questions are invitations to personal encounters with the King of kings. As you respond to His voice by drawing ever closer to Him, He leads you into the center of His will. He asks His questions *for your sake*, not because He does not know the answer. He is challenging you to seek the answers that will bring about the revelation and transformation you need to fulfill your destiny in Christ.

God's questions enable you to move from a position of ordinary life into an extraordinary relationship with Him, which subsequently allows you to experience renewal, restoration, revival, victory, hope, healing, and a greater confidence. His questions also release a greater revelation of Himself, His ways, and matters in which you had no prior knowledge or understanding. The process of eternal transformation is set in motion by a personal encounter with God and a revelation of truth. Understanding truth is foundational for sustained freedom.

God's questions are for the purpose of calling His people back to Himself after they have gone astray. In the book of Micah, He sternly addressed the children of Israel through His prophet.

Introduction

Chiding His people for their great idolatry against Him and their great injustice toward others, God asked through Micah, "My people, what have I done to you? How have I burdened you? Answer me" (Micah 6:3).

In the New Testament, Jesus responded to questions from the leaders of His day with questions of His own. He often conversed with the elite religious men of His time, mainly the chief priests and elders. Jesus seized almost every opportunity to ask them questions, which could have potentially moved them to repentance and changed their wrong beliefs and mindsets if they had been open. Instead, they refused to answer Him. In so doing, they continued on the path of rejecting God's will for their lives.

The 31 questions that God or His servants posed brought about growth and strategic, sometimes radical, changes in the lives of certain men and women in Scripture.

These questions are grouped into five parts:

Divine Dialogue
Miracles
Character
Vision
Authority

As you read through these questions, I pray you will be led to answer each of them for the benefit of your personal revelation and transformation with the Lord. May your relationship with Him grow and mature as you allow the Holy Spirit to reveal the answers from a personal standpoint.

Remember, the questions are *for your sake* and growth. Let your time with Him grow and develop as you walk closer to Him.

PART ONE

QUESTIONS OF DIVINE DIALOGUE

In this section, we will explore the topic of God's questions and look at His purposes and intentions in asking them. We will also examine the importance of a leader's proper response to Him and address the subject of personal encounters with God that result in lasting transformation.

ONE

Will You Give Me a Drink?

> When a Samaritan woman came to draw water, Jesus said to her, "Will you give me a drink?"
>
> *John 4:7*

As the disciples traveled with Jesus through Samaria, they were unaware that Jesus had another agenda. He knew that He would be meeting with one special woman. Upon arriving at a well outside of a small town, Jesus' disciples went into town to find food while Jesus stayed back. While it looked as if He was just resting, He was waiting for her to come. Notice that He waited *for* her. Jesus knew about the impending, life-changing encounter she was about to have, while she had no idea.

Jesus took the initiative to meet this woman. He chose to go to Samaria, and He chose to wait for this one desperately needy woman who approached the well in the heat of the day.

When the woman arrived at the well, Jesus asked a simple question: "Will you give me a drink?" Instead of offering Him a drink, she replied, "You are a Jew, and I am a Samaritan—so how can you ask me for a drink?" According to tradition, Jews did not even use cups and bowls that had been handled by Samaritans. They had ostracized Samaritans for generations, and the Samaritans naturally resented being treated like second-class citizens. There was deep, historical wounding between these two people groups, and the woman let this prejudice carry into her conversation with Jesus. When she first encountered Jesus, pain, division, and shame were the lenses through which she saw Him.

At the end of this unexpected encounter, Jesus freed the Samaritan woman from the bondage that had kept her enslaved. What we want to focus on is *how* He did this. Jesus desired to reveal Himself to the Samaritan woman, but first she needed to be cleansed of all that stood in the way. Scripture tells us that without a pure heart no man can see God, so Jesus poured out living water to cleanse her and bring her into freedom (see Matthew 5:8).

Just what is it that Jesus did?

First, He led her to forgive others. Until we are willing to release all unforgiveness, it is impossible for us to experience true encounters that result in lasting reformation of our life and ministry. Forgiveness is of grave importance, and it is no small matter to God. We must deal with offenses we have harbored and our grievances with other people. When we do so, God will grant us much grace to forgive.

Second, Jesus asked the Samaritan woman to give Him what she thought she needed the most—a drink. He asked her for something, and He will do the same with you. As you give to Him, you position yourself to receive back from Him, aligning yourself to receive all He has. As you receive, you are now in position for your needs to be met. You do not have to live in the scarcity of your situation. Jesus knows your needs and longs to meet them in His way and timing.

Third, Jesus shared that He had living water (see verse 14). The woman at the well, accustomed to the well water and her old ways of living, had no point of reference for living water. During this trip to the well, she had not expected to receive a gift that would meet and satisfy her deepest spiritual needs. In order to receive, however, she was required to act. Giving Him a cup of water was the act of faith and obedience He wanted to see.

Finally, Jesus asked the woman to call her husband. The woman admitted she had no husband, and Jesus revealed that He knew that she had been in five marriages and was currently living in adultery—a very serious situation. As she moved toward Him spiritually, He removed her spiritual blindness. As she met His requests, she was filled with the gift of God, the living water. He liberated her so that she would be able to step confidently and freely into her future, no longer living in regret.

The Lord's questions during times of spiritual encounter will expose our deepest spiritual needs. He wants to help us identify our spiritual condition to lead us to a place of restoration and transformation. His kindness and mercy will lead us to repentance (see Romans 2:4). Transformation begins with an admission of our failures, our shortcomings, and repentance from all our sinful behaviors.

Jesus helped this woman move from a place of shame, embittered by old wounding and prejudices, into true worship and an eternal relationship with the living Savior. She was transformed. The living water within her spirit began to spring up when He revealed Himself to her, saying, "I, the one speaking to you—I am he" (John 4:26).

Life as she had known it was over. Her revelation of the Messiah led her to an impartation of a new life, new vision, new purpose, new hope, new power, and much higher level of commitment to her city and nation. Because of His love for her and the plan He had for her life, He worked through every issue she raised to bring her to a place of personal transformation.

Her perspective and values changed. She reached out to give instead of reaching out to get, and she brought others to partake of the gift she had received. She stopped looking to the same old sources to meet her needs. The liberated Samaritan woman no longer needed to hide from her neighbors in shame. Instead, she came out of hiding to share the living water others around her desperately needed. Jesus shifted her entire life and her eternity. He does the same for you today.

Divine intervention feels unexpected because God works on His timetable to fulfill His purposes in your life. You may be surprised by the encounter, but it has been His plan all along.

The Samaritan woman's life is a picture of your story. God continues to work as He did with His precious Samaritan daughter. He is removing any reproach and setting you free so that you, too, can announce His goodness to those with whom you have influence.

The time is now for us to declare the truth of the One who is the answer for every human dilemma. Jesus waits for you at your well of hurt, tradition, religion, shame, reproach, self-loathing, racism, lack, bondage, abandonment, and every dark place in your soul. He eagerly waits to set you free. He showed the Samaritan woman where the root of her problem was so that she could choose to receive lasting freedom, and He will show you as well. Imagine how He can change your life if you meet Him at your well and give Him your past, failures, fears, doubts, successes, dreams, wishes, and desires in exchange for a life-changing encounter with Him. Come clean before Him. He knows it all anyway. The freedom you will experience is beyond anything you have ever felt.

He loves you! This is your time to receive His living water, to enter the season where all your needs and desires will be met.

What is your "well" of great need?

_____

_____

_____

What is God asking of you? How will you respond to Him?

Do you have old offenses you are holding against someone?

Are you willing to forgive others to move into full restoration and freedom?

Jesus received this woman's full confession. Are you ready to confess it all to Him, too?

TWO

Why Do You Cry?

"Woman, why are you crying?"
John 20:15

In 1625, English essayist Sir Francis Bacon wrote, "A sudden, bold, and unexpected question doth many times surprise a man, and lay him open."*

A well-timed question in the midst of an everyday conversation can catch you off guard and cause you to feel vulnerable, or "laid open," as Sir Francis would say. Certainly, when God poses a question, how much more "laid open" can you be? Like a skilled surgeon, God knows how to slice into the heart of what is ailing your soul and get to the root of the problem. His questions can bring you to wholeness and healing.

After His resurrection, Jesus first appeared to Mary outside the tomb (see John 20). Mary and the other disciples of Jesus were in deep despair and shock. Even though Jesus had told them many times what was going to happen, they were still stunned by His arrest and crucifixion. All hope seemed lost.

---

* Francis Bacon, *The Essays of Francis Bacon: The Fifty-Nine Essays Complete* (Adansonia Publishing, 2018), 80.

The Bible tells us that early in the morning on the first day of the week, Mary went to Jesus' tomb. She was bringing additional embalming oils and spices to make sure that Jesus' body was properly prepared for burial. She was horrified when she discovered that the stone that had covered Jesus' tomb had been moved and that His body was gone. In a panic, she ran to tell Peter and John. They ran to the tomb and found it just as Mary had said. He was, indeed, gone, and only His burial and linen graveclothes remained.

Mary stayed at the tomb while Peter and John returned to the place where the disciples were hiding. She was devastated. Not only had the Messiah been brutally executed, but now His body was gone. Why? Where had it been taken? Weeping, Mary once again inspected the empty tomb, perhaps to convince herself that His body was indeed gone and that this was not some horrible dream. As she turned to leave, she saw a man standing before her. "He asked her, 'Woman, why are you crying? Who is it you are looking for?'" (John 20:15).

Mary did not recognize the man at first, supposing Him to be the gardener. Yet when He called her by her name, she knew immediately. She exclaimed, "Teacher!" and fell at His feet to worship Him (see verse 16).

Something happens deep within our hearts when we hear our Creator, our Father, speaking our name. Upon hearing the sound of her name from the lips of her Savior, Mary fell on her face in total abandonment and worship. Hearing Jesus speak her name removed doubt, fear, and confusion from her soul. The voice that stilled the wind and waves spoke to her broken heart and brought healing. Mary's hope returned after she heard Him speak her name. The devastation was gone. He was alive!

Spiritual dialogues begin with hearing God's voice and responding to His call. Because of a personal encounter, Mary carried a powerful message back to her sphere of influence. Mary announced Jesus' resurrection to His disciples. Through Jesus' questions, they were transformed by an intimate, personal dialogue with Him, and they became very effective in serving His purpose in their generation.

Jesus also asked two important questions: Why are you crying? and Who are you looking for? Those questions opened Mary's heart before the Lord and allowed Him access to heal her.

"Why are you crying?" Was this a gentle question asking Mary why she hadn't believed what she had been told throughout Jesus' ministry? He had promised His followers many times that He would be executed and rise again, and yet He found her weeping and in despair. Was this a marker to her heart that what Jesus said could be trusted?

"Who are you looking for?" Again, could this be a loving wake-up call? Why was Mary looking for Jesus among the dead when He had promised He would return after His death? Perhaps this could be another reminder of the faith we can have in what He says to us, even in the darkest of circumstances. He keeps His promises. Through Jesus' questions, Mary received renewed hope and joy.

Throughout the Bible, we see accounts of God's people responding to His voice and their lives shifting forever. Abraham, "the father of many nations" (Romans 4:18), was instructed by God to leave his country, his people, and his father's household. He obeyed the voice of God and went to a land with which he was unfamiliar (see Genesis 12:1).

Later in Abraham's life, the voice of the Lord tested him once again.

> He said to him, "Abraham!" "Here I am," he replied. Then God said, "Take your son, your only son, whom you love—Isaac—and go to the region of Moriah. Sacrifice him there as a burnt offering on a mountain I will show you."
>
> Genesis 22:1–2

At the end of this passage in Genesis, you will read that Abraham was prepared to obey God's command. At the last moment, however, God provided another sacrifice. Abraham's son was spared, and God blessed Abraham for his obedience. His encounters with God positioned him for covenant blessings and released generational blessings on his descendants.

In the gospel of Luke, we see the story of Zacchaeus, a chief tax collector. Word spread that Jesus was making His way through Zacchaeus' town. Zacchaeus desired to see Jesus when He passed by, but due to his small stature, he had to climb a tree to see the Lord over the crowds. "When Jesus reached the spot, he looked up and said to him, 'Zacchaeus, come down immediately. I must stay at your house today'" (Luke 19:5).

In response to the Lord's call, Zacchaeus left his perch in the sycamore tree and took Jesus to his home. Not only was this man's life changed by Christ that day, but the lives of those in his household were also changed. Jesus said, "Today salvation has come to this house, because this man, too, is a son of Abraham" (Luke 19:9). It all started with Jesus' call and Zacchaeus' response.

A personal encounter with God gives life a brand-new meaning. Have you let yourself be transformed by the voice, love, and power of your Savior? He speaks to you! He's calling your name. He asks you questions not in reprimand but to remind you of who He is. He's waiting for you now with open arms. Don't wait any longer. Run to Him!

Have you heard God call your name?

Have you had a personal encounter with the Lord?

If so, how has your life been changed or affected?

Are you serving God and sharing your testimony?

THREE

Why Do You Persecute Me?

> As he [Saul] neared Damascus on his journey, suddenly a light from heaven flashed around him. He fell to the ground and heard a voice say to him, "Saul, Saul, why do you persecute Me?"
>
> *Acts 9:3–4*

Let's examine the Lord's interactions with a man in the New Testament who went from being an enemy of the Gospel to one who would further the Word of God more than any other apostle. This man's name was Saul, and he held incredible prestige, power, and religious influence in Jerusalem.

Saul was journeying to the city of Damascus with the purpose of locating and imprisoning the followers of Jesus. "But Saul, still breathing threats and murder against the disciples of the Lord, went to the high priest" (Acts 9:1 ESV). Paul was a legalistic and respected religious man who had anger and hatred in his heart. He was on a mission to silence Jesus' followers forever—and he had the backing of the high priest.

While Saul was on the road to Damascus, he had a jarring personal encounter with Jesus Christ that would forever change his life and the lives of billions in the ages to follow. If you have read through some of the books of the New Testament, this man's life has directly had an impact on your life. God's design for Saul would make him one of the most influential New Testament apostles in all of Church history—a purpose ordained long before his birth. For the Lord's plans to be fulfilled, however, God needed to interrupt Saul's everyday life with a question.

A blinding light flashed around Saul, and he fell to the ground (see Acts 9:3–4). Then, a voice said to him, "Saul, Saul, why are you persecuting Me?" Can you imagine the shock and fear Saul must have felt in that moment? It would be as if you were on your way to work and a huge flash of light suddenly sent you flying from your vehicle, and then a booming voice spoke to you. That would certainly get your attention.

Saul responded to the Lord's question with a question of his own: "Who are you, Lord?" (verse 5). Isn't it interesting that Saul knew he was speaking with a "Lord," a divine being, even though he had previously denounced Jesus and all His teachings? Recognizing the lordship of Jesus is the first step toward a lasting, personal transformation.

The Lord answered Saul's question with a statement: "I am Jesus, whom you are persecuting" (verse 5).

Jesus wanted Saul to know His nature, so He revealed Himself as the Messiah. Jesus is a name Saul would have known because Saul was hunting down the followers of Jesus. In essence, Jesus was saying, "I'm Jesus, the one you have been denying, the one whose children you have been imprisoning and killing." This encounter brought Paul face-to-face with the reality of Christ and His existence.

The second half of the Lord's statement identified that He was the one Paul was persecuting. This must have been horrifying for Saul because he was part of the religious elite. In an attempt to please God, he had been actively persecuting Christians in the name of God. He didn't just hate the early Christians because of personal bias—he truly believed he was doing the work of God. Now Jesus, the Son of God, appeared before him and stood in defense of the very people Saul was seeking to annihilate in the name of religion. Talk about finding out you were on the wrong side!

Jesus is kind, because even in our moments of absolute conviction and accountability, He does not leave us to wallow in shame. He said to Paul, "Now get up and go into the city, and you will be told what you must do" (verse 6). Saul discovered he was completely blind. His travel companions lifted this once proud man from the ground, and he was led by the hand into the city to wait for further instruction (see verse 8).

Did you notice something strange? Saul didn't answer the original question Jesus posed to him. Jesus had asked, "Why do you persecute me?" That question was never answered; however, that wasn't the point of Jesus' asking it. The point was to bring Saul face-to-face with the reality of Christ and His existence. Saul didn't realize as he stumbled into Damascus blind, humbled, and terrified that he would be instrumental in laying the foundation for the New Testament Church—the very Church he had sworn to eradicate.

After his encounter, Saul waited in the darkness without food for three days. A disciple in Damascus named Ananias was sent by God to pray for Saul (see verses 10–19). Saul's blindness lifted, and he received both the Holy Spirit and his new name: Paul. God used Ananias to pray for the restoration of Saul's sight, but the implications of his healing went much deeper. Not only was Paul's physical sight restored, but his spiritual eyes were opened, and he was able to see his life from God's perspective.

Paul fully committed himself to Christ and the purposes of God from that day forward. He lived a life of uncompromising obedience to his Master. As we study the account of Paul's life and ministry, we discover that he based his life on the concept that he was not his own, but the possession of Christ. By saying yes to the one he met on the road to Damascus, Paul accepted the lordship of Jesus, His saving grace, and His divine authority for true spiritual leadership. Accepting Christ changed Paul's life and his allegiance forever. The truth of the resurrected Christ and His lordship was forever settled in Paul's heart. How incredible!

An authentic, personal dialogue with the living God will open your spiritual eyes and give you a clear vision of your path and your God-given destiny. The Lord loves to open your eyes, which enables you to discern and see spiritual matters much more clearly. He also has plans for your life that require you to submit your own plans and desires for something even greater. Sometimes, you can move full steam ahead in one direction and think you are walking in God's will, but His plan and His truths are what you need to hear. The questions He asks you in those moments are often some of the most important.

Lay down your own agenda to embrace His. If you truly desire to know Him and what He has destined you to be, you must allow Him access into your life.

Like Paul, let's answer God's questions with our obedience and trust.

Is He prompting the "why" question in your life?

_____

_____

_____

Is He asking why you are doing something or why you are not doing something else?

_____

_____

_____

Are you cooperating with Him, or are you resisting His plan?

Have you asked God what *His* plan/destiny is for your life?

Are you willing to submit to His plan fully?

FOUR

Where Are You?

> But the LORD God called to the man, "Where are you?"
> *Genesis 3:9*

In Genesis, we read that God created Adam and then breathed into him the breath of life (see Genesis 2:7). Adam bore the image and likeness of God and possessed the life-giving Spirit of the Almighty. Man was designed to be a container of the Holy Spirit. This foundational element of his existence, God's Spirit residing within him, is what qualified Adam to have a relationship with Him and gave Adam the authority to rule the earth.

But that isn't where the story ends. In Genesis 3, we observe the most gut-wrenching plot twist in human history. Adam and Eve sinned and fell from their rightful position with God. As a result of that sin, they stepped out from under His protection and blessing—and out of their purpose. By their choice, they removed themselves from following the destiny God had for them and their descendants, spiraling the rest of humanity into opposition with heaven.

In Genesis 3:9, we find Adam and his wife, Eve, hiding in shame after committing the first sin because they realized they were naked. Filled with shame, they hid from God. As the Lord God moved through the Garden, He called to the man.

Why would He call for Adam? To punish him? To chase him down like an angry parent looking to discipline a wayward child? No. Because God's supreme desire and purpose for creating humans was to be in a relationship with them. He wanted to spend time with them. The Garden was the Father's gift to His newly created son and daughter.

This was not just about relationship. It was also about divine purpose. You can read that God created mankind (male and female) on day six of the creation account—the final day before God rested (see Genesis 1:26–31). The use of numbers in the Bible is usually symbolic, and six is a number in Scripture that often symbolizes man or humanity. You could take it even further and add six (Adam) plus six (Eve) to equal twelve, the number indicative in Scripture of governmental perfection. Twelve is the number connected with government, whether by tribes or apostles, in measurement of time, or in things that have to do with government in the heavens and earth. It applies to divine and apostolic governments.[*]

Let us look at these concepts side by side. Mankind was created for the overarching purpose of ruling and reigning with God on the earth (see Genesis 1:26–28). God's desire was for relationship, and His ultimate purpose for mankind was to rule the earth and cause it to function like heaven in cooperation with Him. He made you like Himself, with all the authority necessary to dominate earth, nature, and the rest of creation. Just to clarify, this position of authority does not include domination over fellow human beings; God, not you or me, is supreme over humans.

After Adam's fall, God's initial question centered on relationship, because relationship is God's first priority. It is vital that we understand this. Relationship is His priority. It must also be yours

---

[*] Vivian Bricker, "What Does the Number 12 Mean in the Bible?," Christianity.com, April 25, 2023, https://www.christianity.com/wiki/bible/what-does-the-number-12-mean-in-the-bible.html.

if you are to make any sort of impact on earth for His Kingdom. As messy, hurtful, and complicated relationships and people can be in our fallen state, they are at the forefront of God's heart. This is apparent in Genesis 3:9 because Adam had committed the first sin causing the initial divide between the Almighty and His creation. God's first question, however, was not, "What did you do?" His question was, "Where are you?"

When God asked Adam "Where are you?" it was not because Adam was missing and God couldn't find him in the Garden. It was an invitation to Adam to return to interaction with God. This was the Father's attempt to reestablish their connection for the sake of the relationship. Even today, when we are in sin or have wandered away, God pursues us for the purpose of reconciliation. How loving and beautiful is the heart of God toward His children!

Your purpose is to give God what He desires, and your honor is to be in relationship with Him. You must make it your aim to worship Him wholeheartedly by allowing Him to accomplish His will in and through your life. You must concentrate on drawing close to Him and walking in the full calling He has assigned to you. Be forewarned—to skip the process of building a foundational relationship with God will lead to the abortion of His plans for your life. Without His Spirit, power, and direction, you will be operating in your own strength.

This was a factor in Adam and Eve's sin. They believed they could operate independently of God and receive the knowledge of good and evil (see Genesis 3:5). That choice led to the abortion of their purpose and calling. You must walk in relationship first. Seek Him first. Have no other gods before Him. Align yourself, first and foremost, with your Creator. Get to know Him!

The enemy constantly seeks to cause breaks in your relationship with God because he knows it disrupts God's first priority. You open the door for trouble when you succumb to temptation or attempt to strong-arm God's promises into your life. If you go beyond the boundaries He gives, you open doors for all sorts of evil, as you have no authority in realms to which you have not been assigned. We will flourish and be satisfied only in our own divinely assigned territory, and we learn our place and purpose through a relationship with God.

While Adam and Eve maintained their rightful position before God and operated from their ordained position, they had open communication and fellowship with God. But after their disobedience in the Garden, Adam and Eve hid themselves from God. Something shifted.

The process of becoming all you were meant to be begins with your relationship with your Maker, and the following process is an ongoing, transformational trek. God always has been and always will be concerned about man's proper position in relationship to Himself. His eternal plan for mankind has not changed. It is still His ultimate desire for you to be relationally right with Him (in righteousness) spiritually and in every other sense. In order to accomplish your divinely appointed destiny, you must be correctly positioned and aligned with the King.

The fall of man separated us from God for eternity. The relationship was severed until Jesus came to earth and was crucified and then raised to life again as an atonement for our sin. Jesus' mission in coming to earth was to restore us to the place of perfect relationship with the Father. Restoration is costly, and it would cost the Son of God His life to restore the relationship between God and man. Isn't it a beautiful relief to know that God believed a relationship with you was worth the cost?

When God sees that your heart is for Him, that He is your one desire and that His will is what you want most, He will give you more than you could ask for or even imagine, according to the power of the Holy Spirit working within you (see Ephesians 3:20).

I challenge you to stop hiding from God. Take time to get alone with God. Ask Him to reveal anything and everything that stands in the way of vital, intimate fellowship with Him. He will draw you closer to Himself and show you those things that are in the way. He loves you, and His plans for you are great. The Word declares that when we draw near to Him, He draws near to us (see James 4:7).

When you are rightly aligned with God, He will reveal Himself to you and teach you how to be who you are called to be. God's question is not related to what you have done, but where you are. God's ultimate question to us is this:

"Where are you in our relationship?"

God is calling you—will you hear Him and respond?

Ask yourself, "Am I in the right place?"

"Am I praying according to God's will, or according to my own?"

_____

_____

_____

"Am I committed to building God's Kingdom or my own?"

_____

_____

_____

FIVE

Where Is Your Spouse?

"Where is your wife Sarah?"
Genesis 18:9

Throughout Scripture, you will see how deeply God values family, and how He sets biblical marriage as the core foundation for human relationship. Effective relational leadership begins in the home before it appears in the Church (see Genesis 2:23–25). Ministry also begins at home as you respond to the needs of your family.

God values relationships so much that His plan from the beginning was that man live and thrive in a covenant relationship with Him. He sought out those who would also desire that relationship with Him. God is incredibly relational.

You can see this in the beginning with Adam in the Garden of Eden. From the day they were created, Adam and Eve were positioned for unity and authority together and with God. God spoke blessings and promise over them and granted them authority (see Genesis 1:28). The blessings He spoke over them were designed to be made manifest as the two walked together in one accord. God's intent was for them to become fruitful (through success) and increase (through multiplication) so that they could faithfully rule over all that God had given them. Adam was created to carry the glory of God and to fulfill His purpose by ruling the earth. But because of Adam's disobedience and rebellion, God's original plan for mankind's success did not come to pass. He needed to call upon someone else.

Many years after Adam's death, God called Abram, later called Abraham, to be the father of a new covenant nation. When God called Abraham and Sarah, He spoke promises and blessings over them just as He had with Adam and Eve. The Lord vowed to bless them and make them a blessing to the nations of the world. He also promised to give them a son (see Genesis 17:15–27), which was a miraculous and unbelievable promise, considering Sarah had been barren her whole life, and now they were both elderly. Abraham and Sarah waited over two decades for the Lord to fulfill His promise to them. Twenty-four years later, God returned to visit Abraham and Sarah. He looked around and said to Abraham, "Where is your wife Sarah?" (Genesis 18:9).

No matter how spiritual or successful you might be in your own eyes or in the estimation of others, God is highly concerned with the relationships you have with your spouse and family. When you are in a healthy and godly relationship with the family He has given you, you will be positioned to receive more of what God has promised. Many of the blessings He has for you can only be received when your relationships are God-honoring. This is because His design for your relationships is not just to bring you comfort, joy, and companionship. He designed relationships to shape you more into His likeness and to sanctify you so that you are equipped to bear the blessings and calling on your life.

God pays more attention to our relationships than most of us would like to believe. Each of us has been given the responsibility of knowing how to minister and serve our spouse and our family. It is only from a place of healthy family relationships that we will be able to fulfill His purposes and release His blessings.

What was God really saying to Abraham when He inquired about his wife? Sarah was not with Abraham when God visited the second time; she was inside the tent, while Abraham was outside. Abraham had formerly complained to God about not having children, and he spoke as though he assumed his relative Eliezer would be his heir (see Genesis 15). The Lord corrected his faulty assumption by reaffirming to Abraham that his own son, who would come from his very body, would be the heir of his entire inheritance.

Abraham and Sarah were very old, even by the standards of their day, and they were well past childbearing years. "And so from this one man, and he as good as dead, came descendants as numerous as the stars in the sky and as countless as the sand on the seashore" (Hebrews 11:12).

It must have been hard for Abraham to put aside his natural doubts as he grew older each year with no sign of the promised son. But God was aware of that, which is why, when He first visited Abraham with this incredible promise, He told Abraham to count the stars filling the black night sky. This was an impossible task, as there simply were too many. Can you imagine that first encounter as God and Abraham stood together? Maybe God leaned over as Abraham craned his neck to stare at the countless specks of light against the dark canvas and whispered with anticipation, "So shall your offspring be" (Genesis 15:5).

Can you also imagine how, during the two decades of waiting, Abraham often refreshed his memory of God's promise by looking up to the starry heavens? How many nights did this man of God sit outside his tent in the cool of the evening to receive fresh revelation of God's promise, which in turn strengthened his faith?

But where was Sarah? What was her experience as she waited for a child to come from her ninety-year-old womb? Did Sarah, who was called by God to be the mother of nations, feel unsupported by her husband when she needed to receive strength and renewed faith from the promises of God? Where was Abraham's ministering leadership for his wife? He was outside gathering strength for himself.

Paul wrote of Abraham's faith:

Without weakening in his faith, he faced the fact that his body was as good as dead—since he was about a hundred years old—and that Sarah's womb was also dead. Yet he did not waver through unbelief regarding the promise of God, but was strengthened in his faith and gave glory to God, being fully persuaded that God had power to do what he had promised.

Romans 4:19–22

When God returned to speak to Abraham the second time, He asked Abraham where his wife was because Abraham had not helped Sarah stay strong in faith. It very well could have been a chastisement of this husband who had not been leading and ministering to the needs of his wife. Since Abraham didn't show her the stars and her faith had not been maintained, she encouraged him to marry Hagar and create Ishmael. The war started in Abraham's home and is still going on today.

How does this have an impact on you and me? I seriously challenge you to take a look at your relationship with your spouse and be honest with yourself. Husbands specifically, where is your wife? Where is the woman you are meant to lead and support? If you are a woman, consider these same questions in respect to your relationship with your husband, your family, and the Lord. He has knit you and your husband together as a team.

If you are unmarried, please reflect on your relationship with the family member or person who is closest to you. He or she does not have to be a blood relative. If you have come from a broken home and have surrounded yourself with a new chosen family, you can consider them. This is for the people God has given you as your family.

Let's do an inventory together. Where does your dearest and closest relationship stand?

Spiritually: Where is your family member in relation to his or her faith, hopes, dreams, and walk with the Lord? Do you know what his or her deepest desires and aspirations are? Have you been, or are you, willing to support his or her spiritual growth?

Relationally: Are your family members blossoming in their social lives with their friendships, etc.? How are their relationships with their children? How is the relationship between you and them?

Professionally: Is your spouse or closest friend or family member fulfilled in his or her career? Is he or she using the gifts and talents he or she has been given?

Physically: Are they able to remain healthy and energetic? Is there anything you could do to support them as they create healthy habits?

Financially: Is your family member feeling financially secure?

SIX

Where Is Your Brother?

> Then the LORD said to Cain, "Where is your brother Abel?"
> *Genesis 4:9*

After Adam and Eve were cast out of the Garden of Eden (see Genesis 3:23–24), they had two sons, Cain and Abel. The verse above is incredibly important because it was the scene of the first murder recorded in human history. Cain murdered his younger brother, Abel, one day after he was prompted to violence by a spirit of jealousy. The Lord came to Cain much in the same way He had approached Cain's father, Adam, in the Garden of Eden after the Fall. He searched for the man, and when He found him, He asked, "Where is your brother Abel?"

The Lord knew, of course, that Abel had been slain by Cain. He asked the question because He wanted to make it clear that He held Cain accountable for the care of his younger sibling. Cain's response was "'I don't know,' he replied. 'Am I my brother's keeper?'" (Genesis 4:9). Cain replied to God's question with a question that sprung from his bitter heart. But why was he so filled with anger and jealousy?

This was not the Lord's first conversation with Cain. Prior to this exchange, Cain had presented the Lord with a sacrificial offering that God found unacceptable because it had not come from a heart of worship. Cain was deeply wounded by this rejection and took it very personally.

On the other hand, Abel offered a sacrifice that pleased the Lord (see Genesis 4:3–5). The Lord is a good Father, so He explained to Cain why He found his offering unacceptable.

> Then the LORD said to Cain, "Why are you angry? Why is your face downcast? If you do what is right, will you not be accepted? But if you do not do what is right, sin is crouching at your door; it desires to have you, but you must rule over it."
>
> Genesis 4:6

Cain did not care about growing or ruling over his sin nature. He began to compare himself with Abel, which set him on a self-destructive path that culminated in murdering his brother. Whenever you are driven by jealousy, you will end up destroying what you are building. As leaders, we are accountable to God for the lives of those we lead. This obligation includes watching over their physical, social, professional, and spiritual development. Consider that the first murder recorded in human history was prompted by a spirit of jealousy. Cain killed not only another leader but his brother.

When we compare, we open ourselves up to all sorts of evil. The product of comparison is usually evil fruit such as anger, hatred, rage, jealousy, distrust, resentment, and envy. Indeed, the roots of anger, desperation, and despair can be traced to spirits of fear, jealousy, and pride. When you are operating under the influence of such demonic forces, you will find it difficult to come to the Lord in confession and repentance, which in turn keeps you isolated, in a vulnerable place, and more open to the enemy.

Negative emotions not only hinder you from moving forward in God's plan for your life, but can be relationally debilitating. If left for long periods of time, they will destroy your relationships. You will not be free to walk in the love of God in which He called us to walk.

So what does the Lord require of you and me? God's will is that you attend to the needs of your family and nurture others to grow and mature into the full stature of Christ. The apostle Paul wrote about this familial responsibility (see 1 Timothy 5:4, 8, 16). Paul taught that leading and managing the matters of one's household qualifies one to lead others (see 1 Timothy 3:4–5).

You must be hypervigilant to guard against becoming overly busy with "good" things and forsaking those who are to be your priority. Babysitters, friends, peers, teachers, coaches, and other family members (except in extenuating circumstances) are no substitutions for parents. The wounding and pain caused by a lack of care may cause irreparable damage. Have you ever considered the whereabouts of Adam and Eve while the relational strife with their sons was going on? They were neglectful in this respect, as they failed to recognize and address the state of affairs.

God deeply desires for you to care for the people He has given to you to steward. Whether they are a family member, spouse, mentee, colleague, friend, or child, God cares about how you care for those people. The writer of the book of Hebrews summarized it this way: "Obey your leaders and act under their authority. They are watching over you, because *they are responsible for your souls*" (Hebrews 13:17 NCV, emphasis added).

In the Old Testament, leaders were viewed as shepherds of the people. Another name could be caretakers. The heart of a shepherd is to tenderly lead and nurture those under his care. There are many examples in the Bible of shepherding, including 2 Samuel 5:2, 7:7 and Isaiah 44:28. Jesus Christ, of course, is the ultimate Shepherd, as stated in John 10:11. Jesus set the standard for those of us who would join Him as shepherds of His people (see 1 Peter 5:2–4).

You have a responsibility to pray for and counsel the people around you in an appropriate manner when problems arise. This doesn't mean they won't still make wrong choices and go their own way if they choose, but you will have done what is right in the Lord's eyes.

Jesus referred to this manner of care when He, at the end of His life, prayed to His Father about the future of those He had shepherded. "While I was with them, I protected them and kept them safe by that name you gave me" (John 17:12). He protected them at the expense of His own life (see John 18:8–9). Today's leaders are often more concerned about managing the intangibles than managing the individuals under their authority, while God's aim for us is to care for the people over whom we have been given charge.

Make no mistake—effective relational leadership stems from a love relationship with the Father. You are able to serve others well once you have received revelation of His love for them. As a member of the Father's Kingdom family, you are to follow Christ's example of relating to others from this paradigm (see Ephesians 2:19). As a lover of God and carrier of His heart, you are filled and empowered by Him to act in the best interest of others.

Love God first, and then love others as you love yourself. Loving our brothers and sisters in the Lord is very rewarding, both in the natural and in the spiritual realm.

Are you in a leadership role? Are you a parent, boss, etc.?

_____

_____

_____

Do you know how to submit to authority?

_____

_____

Have you experienced God's love for your "brothers" or "family" in the faith?

Have you ever dealt with anger or jealousy? Was the outcome positive or negative?

Do you understand how dangerous these emotions are if not brought under the headship of the Lord Jesus?

SEVEN

What Is Your Name?

> [The Man] asked him, What is your name? And [in shock of realization, whispering] he said, Jacob [supplanter, schemer, trickster, swindler]!
>
> *Genesis 32:27* AMPC

When we meet a person for the first time, we usually ask them, "What is your name?" A name is what distinguishes us from others. It can denote identity, family connection, and much more. An individual's distinct essence, history, and personality are declared through his or her name, and it serves as a marker for belonging.

In biblical times, names held far more weight in the culture than they do now. When families named their children, they picked names that expressed their wishes, desires, or hopes for the child's future. Many names served as a parent's prophetic expression of God's will for the life of that child. Names were generally descriptive of a person, his or her position, or some other circumstance affecting that person's life. They also indicated tribal belonging. You will even see throughout the Bible that there were instances where God hand-selected a name for a child before that child was even born. Let's explore this more together.

The first example is found in the book of Genesis. In this passage, Jacob is fleeing from his brother Esau (see 32:7). He has taken all his wives and children, his servants, and some stolen possessions from his father-in-law, Laban. Knowing that Esau was not far away, Jacob ran to hide in the desert. Why should he fear his brother? He had cheated Esau out of his birthright, which was an incredible betrayal in that time (see Genesis 27). He had stolen things that did not belong to him, and he ran to hide. In short, Jacob is a mess in this passage, and the consequences of his deceptive sins are catching up to him. He is panicking, which makes him a man on the run.

The Word describes how Jacob left his camp at night and began wrestling with a strange man (see Genesis 32:24–26). Biblical scholars have debated whether this was Jesus or the angel of the Lord, but all are in agreement that it was not just a normal man who spontaneously started wrestling at night with a guy who was down on his luck. This was an intentional encounter arranged by the Lord to set Jacob on his path to purpose.

As Jacob wrestled with the man, the man asked him, "What is your name?" (see verse 27). Jacob gave the man his name. If you were to do a quick search for the meaning of the name Jacob, it might reveal that the name carries with it many interpretations, including deceiver, swindler, schemer, etc. Given what we know about Jacob's history, it is clear that he had fulfilled the meaning of his name—but that was about to change. The man Jacob had been wrestling with declared, "Your name will no longer be Jacob, but Israel, because you have struggled with God and with humans and have overcome" (verse 28).

For years, Jacob had lived a life of ignorance concerning his identity. As a result of his sinful actions, he had become someone he was never designed to be. In his own strength, he had attempted to become who his spirit man knew he was. But he became someone he was never meant to be.

The man he wrestled with (likely an angel of the Lord) wanted Jacob to see himself in light of who he had become. Jacob needed to see that there was more than what he had experienced to date. So the man gave something to Jacob that he had not anticipated, his true identity. It was as if the Lord put a mirror before Jacob's face and allowed him to see himself. When Jacob saw himself, he was brought to the end of himself. This encounter gave him a priceless gift of knowing who he was. Only through this face-to-face encounter with the Lord was Jacob able to turn his life around.

Jacob had received his prophetic destiny before birth in the form of his original name. He had also received a prophetic dream at Bethel (house of God), and his name of prophetic destiny at Peniel (the face of God), where he wrestled with the man. In truth, Israel was always his identity.

From that day forward, Jacob was known as Israel, and his destiny was changed. An entire nation was named after him as he walked faithfully with the Lord. Jacob's twelve sons went on to lead the twelve tribes of Israel. In the names of his sons, we see representations of prophetic destiny, and each fulfilled those prophetic purposes. Each son's name had a meaning that included the call of God on the son, and something that explained the experience of each mother. Remember that Jacob's wives, Leah and Rachel, also were going through difficult circumstances and conflict throughout the account in Genesis. This was not lost on the Lord; He saw and recognized it. Through the naming of each child, the child's identity was established.

Reuben—See or behold a son (Genesis 29:32)
Simeon—God hears (Genesis 29:33)
Levi—Companion or attached to (Genesis 29:34)
Judah—Praise (Genesis 29:35)

Dan—Vindicated (Genesis 30:6)
Naphtali—Struggled (Genesis 30:8)
Gad—Fortune (Genesis 30:11)
Asher—Happy (Genesis 30:13)
Issachar—Hired (Genesis 30:18)
Zebulun—Exalted, honored (Genesis 30:20)
Joseph—May He add (Genesis 30:24)
Benjamin—Son of the right hand (Genesis 35:18)

The names of Jacob's twelve sons summed up the parents' hopes for each child. When a father and mother are sensitive to God's leading, they will follow His will for their children's lives.

It's not just a task for your parents to name you. God gave you a unique name known only by Himself before you were conceived. That name remains a mystery until He reveals it to each person one day in heaven. Isn't that beautiful? Don't you feel known by the Father? He names you according to your prophetic destiny and purpose in life, and He shares that name only with you. The prophet Isaiah put it this way: "Before I was born the LORD called me; *from my mother's womb he has spoken my name*" (Isaiah 49:1, emphasis added).

When God names an individual, He speaks into existence that person's eternal, prophetic destiny. Ishmael was named before he was born, and his lifestyle and character were described in advance by the angel of the Lord (see Genesis 16:11–12). John the Baptist was named and filled with the Holy Spirit before he was born. His life assignment was described in detail to his father by an angel (see Luke 1:13–17). In fact, the Lord Jesus was named before He came into the world. The angel Gabriel appeared to Mary and gave her a message about His birth and ministry (see Luke 1:30–33; Matthew 1:21).

Names are also relational in nature and grant inherent authority. When a child receives his family's name, he is then qualified for the legacy that comes with that name, and he is awarded the authority necessary to fulfill his birthright. Your name is your passport or identification card that gives you the spiritual right to lead in your area of calling.

Another dimension of naming a person is marking out (designation). The process of marking out separates a leader from a follower. It means to ascribe to a person a level of accountability, responsibility, and visibility. Marking out is one process by which a leader is identified as the one who is—or will be—in charge.

Names of destiny are prophetic and reveal both the purpose of God and His promises in relation to His eternal plan. God is so serious about fulfilling His purposes in the life of an individual that, if need be, He will orchestrate a name change. Here are a few cases in which God chose to rename His servants: Abram to Abraham (see Genesis 17:5), Sarai to Sarah (see Genesis 17:15–16), Jacob to Israel (see Genesis 32:27–28), and Simon to Peter (see John 1:42).

The Lord names a person and then orchestrates his or her life in such a way to lead that person into experiences that will eventually mold him or her into the person who exemplifies the name. God's names represent His desired product.

Walking in your divine identity means operating from a position of strength and confidence in who you are. Once God has made you acutely aware of who you are, no man can take that deep awareness from you. Strength, confidence, and resolve grow from the knowledge of who you are.

Knowing God and knowing yourself are foundational elements in becoming who you are. Only as we come to discover, understand, and fully accept our identity are we able to be successful in fulfilling our God-given destiny.

Do you know what your name means?

What does your family name(s) mean?

Does the meaning correlate to who you know yourself to be?

Can you see God's identity in your name?

EIGHT

Who Are You?

> He asked for a writing tablet, and to everyone's
> astonishment he wrote, "His name is John."
> *Luke 1:63*

> And you, my child, will be called a prophet of the Most High;
> for you will go on before the Lord to prepare the way for him.
> *Luke 1:76*

Who were you called to be? Before you give a title like pastor, doctor, or parent, let me clarify something: Who you are has nothing to do with the titles, roles, or positions you may hold. Who are you in light of your life's assignment given to you by your Father in heaven?

When God breathes an understanding of your identity into your heart, that realization can become like a fire burning deeply within your being. The prophet Jeremiah put it this way as he shared his personal experience: "His word is in my heart like a fire, a fire shut up in my bones" (Jeremiah 20:9).

As you identify the call of God on your life and you embrace and walk in your revealed identity, authority, power, and favor, you will find that every provision necessary to complete your mission is released from the Father. Isn't that incredible? The assignment came from Him, so the power to complete it also rests in Him. The revelation of your identity also liberates you from the limitations of this world and its systems because God knows no limits. If He calls you to it, He will equip you through it, and no force of nature or man can stop His mighty plan.

As you understand more and more who you are and what you were called to do, you can avoid creating a personal identity based on your activities or titles. I hope that knowledge is an instant relief to your spirit. Your *do* is meant to be a result of your *who* and not the other way around. Too many of us, because we have not understood who we are, have contrived a false identity. We have assumed we are what we do. Aren't you glad to hear that *to be* is the essence of true identity?

On the other hand, a deficient, faulty perception of your identity can cause you to gravitate from one extreme to another. You may catch yourself leaning toward pride (an overestimation of yourself) and relying on your own strength to bolster this false identity. Alternatively, you could become extremely insecure (an inferiority complex) and not attempt to be who God made you to be because you don't think you are worthy or capable of the call. Both maladies stem from the same root problem: a dangerous lack of self-knowledge.

You *must* possess a revelation and a strong understanding of who you are in Christ to exercise effective Christian leadership and to be who God calls you to be. The answer to the question of *who* reflects your relationship with God and the prophetic call on your life. When your name is identified and illuminated and when your purpose is understood, you are then capable of living a life worthy of your call.

John the Baptist had no need to question who he was. His parents had received the word of the Lord before John's birth.

They knew who their son was called to be (see Luke 1:13–17). Not only did they receive the word, but John's father, Zechariah, confirmed the word and spoke prophetic confirmation over his son (see verses 67–79). This is interesting, because Zechariah had initially doubted that John would be born at all (see verse 18).

He and his wife, Elizabeth, were far beyond childbearing years, and Elizabeth was barren; however, the angel Gabriel confirmed that Elizabeth would bear a child, he shared what that child's name would be, and he told them what his calling was to be. This is incredible! There is no doubt that John's parents nurtured him in line with that call as he grew and matured.

Zechariah established John's identity by declaring, "You, my child, will be called a prophet of the Most High" (Luke 1:76). This statement simplified and clarified both John's identity and the leadership role he was designed to fulfill. As an adult, John did not need to question who he was as a leader. John's life and authority were a mystery to many and raised questions in the minds of leaders of his time, but because he knew who he was, he did not allow their skepticism to move him from his course. When others tried to label him, he was able to counter invalid assumptions and conjectures with the truth (see John 1:19–27). John's prophetic destiny was to be a prophet of the Most High. He took his assignment very seriously and did not buckle under external pressure from those around him in an attempt to be popular or accepted.

Moses was also a man who knew who he was; therefore, he was able to refuse the temptation of being called the son of Pharaoh's daughter. That identity would have set up Moses' entire life for success, riches, opportunities, power, and authority in one of the greatest empires of the time. Instead, he knew his true identity and chose to be mistreated and abused in abject misery along with the people of God, his Hebrew brothers and sisters (see Hebrews 11:24–28).

Furthermore, during his years of exile in the desert, Moses waited upon the Lord's timing in an attitude of faith. He waited until he was an old man, at which point God confirmed his calling through the burning bush. The revelation of the burning bush propelled Moses to step fully into God's destiny for his life.

Jacob, after a grueling wrestling match with a mysterious man (on what probably felt like the longest night of his life) came face-to-face with God (see Genesis 32:24–28). Jacob cried out, not for the blessing of material wealth or increase, but for the release of the blessing of his destiny. He demanded his blessing, because with blessing came identity. Jacob had had enough of his former identity.

Because of Jacob's ignorance of how God viewed identity, much of his life was spent manipulating and controlling circumstances to achieve what he was already predestined to receive from God. Doesn't that cause you to immediately stop and reflect on your own life? We often try to take the reins from God to steer into the calling He is happy and ready to guide us into. Instead of submitting himself to the Lord, Jacob conspired to bring things about in his own way and by his own methods. There came a point during his wrestling with the man, however, when his eyes were opened to the truth of who he had become and who he was called to be.

There are a number of things you can learn from Jacob's story. First, you need to wait on God and allow Him to reveal to you who you have been and who you need to become in light of His design for your life. Second, you need to trust in God. You can secure titles or positions or jump into things prematurely instead of trusting God to provide and open doors in His timing, but that isn't His best. You may gain the power your carnal nature enjoys, but in doing so, you forego the authority and blessing of God. Third, you need to walk in integrity. If you know and are confident in who you are, you are more likely to live a life of authenticity and transparency.

Jacob obtained his preordained heritage by deceptive means rather than by trusting God to provide it. He "purchased" his destiny instead of waiting on God to give it to him.

We were created to know who, and whose, we are, and we are designed for intimacy and fellowship with our Creator God. He wants us to know who we are and to live from that place to be able to affect the world around us.

How many times have you caught yourself purchasing your destiny instead of waiting on the Lord to bestow what He has promised?

_____

_____

_____

Is your *do* a result of your *who*? Or is it the other way around?

_____

_____

_____

Do you try to earn who you are through your relationships or your own efforts?

_____

_____

_____

Has God revealed to you who you really are?

_____

_____

NINE

Who Do You Say I Am?

> When Jesus came into the region of Caesarea Philippi, He asked His disciples, saying, "Who do men say that I, the Son of Man, am?" So they said, "Some say John the Baptist, some Elijah, and others Jeremiah or one of the prophets." He said to them, "But who do you say that I am?"
>
> *Matthew 16:13–15* NKJV

God created you and breathed life into you not only to carry His image but also to know Him and to make Him known to others. The depth at which you know Him determines how prepared you are for your calling. That depth establishes you for a long-term, effective, and fruitful walk.

Seeking the Lord with all your heart, soul, mind, and spirit doesn't just draw you to the Lord, it also draws God to you. He qualifies you to receive His grace, mercy, and favor, making you a true witness in your generation of His power to save, restore, and reform. Being a true witness means hearing, seeing, and experiencing God by being in His presence to declare His glory and

His marvelous deeds. Seeing and experiencing Him makes your testimony that much more credible.

Since you were created to know God, your core purpose is to abide in His presence daily. The process of abiding in His presence, as well as in His Word, begins first by hearing His voice. In the Old Testament, there is more emphasis on abiding *with* God, and in the New Testament, the emphasis is on abiding *in* God.

In the Old Testament, God came to tabernacle among His people. "Then have them make a sanctuary for me, and I will dwell among them" (Exodus 25:8). In the New Testament, however, He came to dwell in us. "Jesus replied, 'Anyone who loves me will obey my teaching. My Father will love them, and we will come to them and make our home with them'" (John 14:23). Furthermore, Jesus' invitation is for us to abide in Him. "Abide in Me, and I in you" (John 15:4 NKJV). It is impossible, however, to abide with Him and abide in Him without first determining to follow Him.

Where do you start? The mark of a man or woman who is walking with God is the ability to hear His voice and follow Him wholeheartedly with total surrender and a desire to please Him. This means you should be dwelling in His presence and living with Him before you attempt to live for Him. After sin separated us from God, He has continued to look for the kind of person who is ready to truly walk with Him. In fact, He has been looking for that person throughout human history in every generation.

In the first search, after Abel was killed by his jealous brother Cain, God found two men among all humanity who would enter a true relationship with Him. Those two men were Enoch and Noah.

Enoch lived 365 years, and for the last 300 of those years he walked closely with the Lord until God took him home (see Genesis 5:22–24). The Bible also says that Noah was a righteous man who walked with God (see Genesis 6:9). Both men were known for their walks with God. They came to Him and followed Him despite the spiritual depravity of their generation, and they identified themselves as followers of the true God.

In my view, these two were a prophetic picture of what God is looking for in every generation. That was one of the reasons why Jesus said to His first disciples, "'Follow Me, and I will make you fishers of men.' They immediately left their nets and followed Him" (Matthew 4:19–20 NKJV). Jesus asked the disciples to follow Him, not just so that He could have disciples, but also so that He could reveal Himself and the Kingdom to them as God the Father had revealed Himself to Enoch and Noah.

The process of knowing Him at a deeper level includes the following:

1. Following Him to Know Him

Jesus lived according to His prophetic name, and in God's view, a name is not just a label. It is a description of purpose, true prophetic identity, and life's calling. Our prophetic name is in our identity. When we talk about prophetic names, we are not limited to names that have a special meaning in specific languages. Rather, the meaning comes from God's plan and purpose that enables us to let go of everything to follow Him with a desire to also know Him. God's plan and purpose for your life also enables you to let go of everything this world would place on you so that you can follow Him and know Him.

2. Walking with Him to Know Him

It's not what you do for God but what you are willing to be for God. Walking with God requires holiness, full surrender, and dedication to the purposes of God. This is why when the Lord Jesus called His disciples, He secured their full commitment to leave everything and follow Him. It was only after they had been walking with Him for a while that He asked them, "Who do you say I am?" (Matthew 16:15).

Enoch gave up everything to follow God. He willingly separated himself unto God to live a holy life. It was not what he did for God, but what he was willing to be for God that made him remarkably special in the Lord's eyes. Walking with God requires full agreement. "Do two men walk together unless they have made an appointment?" (Amos 3:3 NASB).

3. Surrendering to Know Him

Surrender is more than just an agreement with someone to bow to their will over your life. It is a determination to pay the price, not turn back, and give your all. Enoch decided to surrender to God's will and purpose at the age of 65 years old. He dedicated himself to the Lord regardless of what others in his generation were doing. The Bible doesn't tell us what it cost Enoch to submit to God's plan, but we do know that he didn't want to go back to his life as he had known it for the previous 65 years.

4. Pleasing God

"He was commended as one who pleased God" (Hebrews 11:5). Enoch was praised by God for pleasing God. How did he please God? He walked with Him in close friendship and surrender, walking by faith and trust. He pleased God not by his activities or what he did for God, but through his relationship with the Lord, which is what God desires more than anything in every generation. In fact, the Lord didn't wait to call Enoch home; he just disappeared and went to be with the Lord.

This is also why God declared over the Lord Jesus, "This is my Son, whom I love; with him I am well pleased" (Matthew 3:17). There is no greater victory or reward in human history than to know that you pleased God.

Jesus started His ministry by asking His disciples to follow Him, to walk with Him, and to believe in Him. It is impossible to please God without faith, but it is also impossible to know God without faith. We live, follow, and know Him by faith. "The righteous will live by faith" (Galatians 3:11). Faith is believing what is being revealed to you and acting upon it for a deeper knowledge of God.

This type of walk with God creates a strong desire to know Him. That was one of the reasons why the disciples asked Jesus to show them the character and nature of God the Father. The more they walked with Jesus, the more they wanted to know God. The more we know Him, the easier it gets to let everything else go in order to live for Him.

That was why the Lord Jesus turned to His disciples in Matthew 16:13 and asked, "Who do people say the Son of Man is?" They gave Him a summary report about what they had heard people say about Him. Jesus didn't respond to what people said about Him. He shifted the focus, immediately, from the people to His disciples by saying, "'But what about you?' he asked. 'Who do you say I am?'" (verse 15). The most important thing was not the opinion of the people, but the understanding the disciples had of who He was, since they were called to be His witnesses. The question was not about His work or title, but who He was to them.

In every generation, God has been looking for those who are willing to separate themselves to walk with Him and testify of His goodness. That is what it means to walk with Him in a relationship that honors and glorifies His holy name.

Are you walking with Him?

Do you know Him?

_____

_____

_____

If Jesus asked you, "Who do you say that I am?" what would your response be?

_____

_____

_____

Do you want to know God in a deeper way?

_____

_____

_____

TEN

Do You Believe That I Am Able to Do This?

> When He entered the house, the blind men came up to Him, and Jesus said to them, "Do you believe that I am able to do this?" They said to Him, "Yes, Lord."
>
> *Matthew 9:28* NASB

Without faith there is no life. There is no hope, there is no future, there is no tomorrow, there is no solution for personal or national problems, there is no victory, there is no joy, there is no peace, and there is no meaning to life. Most of all, there is no salvation, since we are saved by grace through faith. We are justified by faith, and we live by faith. "The just shall live by his faith" (Habakkuk 2:4 NKJV).

The first foundation of our Christian life is our faith in who God is. Faith is not our assumptions or wishes—it is standing on what God said and the revelation of the Word of God by the Holy Spirit. This Spirit came to lead us into all truth, since faith comes from hearing. "So then faith comes by hearing, and hearing by the word of God" (Romans 10:17 NKJV).

The second foundational factor for our faith is to believe the word we hear. The source of our faith is in believing the eternal Word of God, which leads us into action by providing a strong foundation for our faith. We can then be grounded in the truth. The Lord Jesus affirmed this when He said, "Therefore everyone who hears these words of mine and puts them into practice is like a wise man who built his house on the rock" (Matthew 7:24). Our faith enables us to focus on who He is, instead of on our circumstances or the situation in which we find ourselves.

Paul said, "For no matter how many promises God has made, they are 'Yes' in Christ. And so through him the 'Amen' is spoken by us to the glory of God" (2 Corinthians 1:20). This is one of the reasons why our focus should always be on Christ.

The angel Gabriel confirmed this when he said to Mary, "For with God nothing is ever impossible and no word from God shall be without power or impossible of fulfillment" (Luke 1:37 AMPC). Elizabeth echoed the same thing by saying, "Blessed is she who has believed that the Lord would fulfill his promises to her!" (Luke 1:45). Believing the Word of the Lord is the master key to receiving our promised blessings. In the context of the story, let's highlight the following:

First, you can believe that Jesus knows and understands the depth of your dedication. "This Mary . . . was the same one who poured perfume on the Lord and wiped his feet with her hair" (John 11:2). When we go through challenging situations or our expectations are not fulfilled, the enemy attacks us with deferred hope. This leads us to doubt the value of our contributions or dedication. In such circumstances, it is very important to remember that God knows and sees everything; nothing is wasted.

Second, you can believe that all things work together for His glory and for your good because of your love for Him. That was the reason why Jesus said, "This sickness will not end in death. No, it is for God's glory so that God's Son may be glorified through it" (John 11:4). Believing and standing on His promises, despite what you see, gives the Lord the opportunity to reveal His glory. As Elisha declared, "This is an easy thing in the eyes of the LORD" (2 Kings 3:18).

Third, you are to believe that His love never changes, regardless of the valley you go through. "Jesus loved Martha and her sister and Lazarus" (John 11:5). The love of God is unconditional and doesn't go up and down. Not only does God give love, but He is love. Believing this truth empowers us to see His glory.

Fourth, you can believe the Lord's timing is always right and perfect, since He makes everything beautiful according to His timetable. When Jesus received the urgent call from Mary and Martha that Lazarus was ill, He didn't come right away. "When he heard that Lazarus was sick, he stayed where he was two more days, and then he said to his disciples, 'Let us go back to Judea'" (John 11:6–7). By the time the Lord Jesus arrived, humanly speaking, it was too late. They had lost hope and had buried him.

We are in a timeline, but the Lord is outside of time. His action is not limited by time, since He is the I AM. As human beings, we are bound by yesterday, today, and tomorrow. Yesterday tries to load us with guilt for what we did or didn't do. Today's challenges can make us lose hope. The worries of tomorrow would like to limit us. The only way we can see His glory is by believing that our days were written in His book before we were born. "All the days ordained for me were written in your book before one of them came to be" (Psalm 139:16). That includes our yesterday, today, and tomorrow. That is how we see His glory!

Fifth, you can believe that the Lord, who created you in His image and saved you for His glory, is still in control of your situation, no matter what it might look like. That is called faith! That is the reason Paul said, "And now these three remain: faith, hope and love. But the greatest of these is love" (1 Corinthians 13:13). The apostle Paul made this summary to encourage and challenge the church in Corinth to live for God and serve Him according to their spiritual gifts.

Faith gives a solid base to live for God, as it molds and shapes your values. This gives the strength to dream about tomorrow with a greater hope. Hope creates an expectancy to live a life worthy of the glory of God by acting upon what you believe. This leads to a life of love for God and others. Your faith enables you to let go of the past to envision the future with greater anticipation so that you can live daily for a greater value: love. These three prepare you to believe the impossible to see His glory.

Sixth, you can believe that Jesus is the answer, since He is the I AM. The answer! The resurrection! The life!

> Jesus said to her, "Your brother will rise again." Martha answered, "I know he will rise again in the resurrection at the last day." Jesus said to her, "I am the resurrection and the life. The one who believes in me will live, even though they die; and whoever lives by believing in me will never die. Do you believe this?"
>
> John 11:23–26

Seventh, if you believe, show me where the problem is. The solution to your problems and challenges is to show them to the Lord. "'Where have you laid him?' he asked. 'Come and see, Lord,' they replied" (John 11:34). Instead of trying to explain where Lazarus was, they took Jesus to the burial place to see. When He comes and sees, the problem is solved because He is the answer.

Eighth, you can believe and remove the stone to see His glory. Your demonstration of faith is your willingness to remove the stone placed by unbelief and the culture. Jesus was willing to raise Lazarus, but first the family needed to deal with the sign of unbelief.

> "Take away the stone," he said. "But, Lord," said Martha, the sister of the dead man, "by this time there is a bad odor, for he has been there four days." Then Jesus said, "Did I not tell you that if you believe, you will see the glory of God?"
>
> John 11:39–40

This is why He said that if you believed, you would see the glory of God. Removing the signs of unbelief will give us a lasting victory.

Ninth, you can believe that nothing is impossible, for the Lord will show you His glory. I am sure that when the Lord Jesus asked where Lazarus was buried, those around Him didn't expect Him to call out a person who had been dead for four days. Jesus stood before the burial stone and praised His Father for hearing Him and then "Jesus called in a loud voice, 'Lazarus, come out!' The dead man came out, his hands and feet wrapped with strips of linen, and a cloth around his face" (verses 43–44). This confirmed what Jesus had said about Himself, "I am the resurrection and the life" (verse 25). This resulted in the salvation of many. "Therefore many of the Jews who had come to visit Mary, and had seen what Jesus did, believed in him" (verse 45).

Finally, you can believe and obey. Mary and Martha's first act of obedience enabled them to remove the stone of unbelief by faith. The second, more importantly, was removing the graveclothes to untie Lazarus' feet and hands and the covering over his face so that he could see. "Jesus said to them, 'Take off the grave clothes and let him go'" (verse 44). This was a sign of total freedom for Lazarus to reflect the glory of God.

If you like to see the glory of God, faith, prayer, and obedience can't be separated! That was the reason Jesus asked those who cried to Him for healing a simple question: "Do you believe that I am able to do this?" (Matthew 9:28). We receive by believing His love, mercy, and power to do what He promised. Hence, when we believe, we receive, see, and live for His glory!

Do you believe?

What do you believe?

___

___

___

Have you used your faith, believed, and received from the Lord?

___

___

___

Are you believing for something right now—standing in faith?

___

___

___

PART TWO

QUESTIONS OF MIRACLES

In Part Two, we will examine God's questions concerning our need for Him to do what only He can do. He is the God of the impossible, and His Word continues to reveal this to us. This happens through the woman with the issue of blood and the blind man who miraculously sees.

ELEVEN

Who Touched My Clothes?

> She thought, "If I just touch his clothes, I will be healed." Immediately her bleeding stopped and she felt in her body that she was freed from her suffering. At once Jesus realized that power had gone out from him. He turned around in the crowd and asked, "Who touched my clothes?"
>
> *Mark 5:28–30*

Why did the all-knowing, omnipotent Jesus ask a crowd of people pushing into Him in a tight space, "Who touched My clothes?" Consider the scene.

Jesus was surrounded by a huge crowd that followed Him and kept pressing Him on all sides. He had been stopped and rerouted already by Jairus, the synagogue leader. Jairus had pushed through this throng of people and thrown himself at the Lord's feet, pleading with Him to come and place His hands on his daughter for healing. Jesus agreed, and the mass of humanity started moving toward Jairus' house. On that day, there was a woman in the crowd who was desperate for healing. She, however, was not looking for the Lord to put His hands upon her for healing and deliverance. She would take less than that. She would take anything.

The crowd was pushing each other to come closer to Jesus, jostling and shoving. In this situation, it might seem like a strange time to ask, "Who touched My clothes?" The disciples answered, "You see the people crowding against you . . . and yet you can ask, 'Who touched me?'" (Mark 5:31).

Their answer could almost be interpreted, "What are You talking about? Can't you see all these people around You?" Jesus, however, continued searching, not for somebody who pushed Him, but for the one person who touched Him by faith.

We don't know her background or her name, but we do know the challenges she faced. She had been bleeding for twelve years with an incurable illness in her innermost parts. Due to the Levitical laws, this woman was considered an outcast until her condition improved. She was forbidden from touching anyone, and no one was allowed to touch her. Can you imagine how it would feel to go twelve years without a kind or loving human touch? Desperate, she had tried everything. She had gone to every expert and used up all her money to find a cure, but the bleeding did not stop. While her situation was very discouraging, she refused to give up. The only things she had was herself and her faith. She had no money, no friends, and no access to resources.

She observed what was happening from afar and had heard that the power of the Lord Jesus could heal and deliver. Since she couldn't talk to anyone else, she began to talk to herself, saying, "If I only touch his cloak, I will be healed" (Matthew 9:21). She knew she was at risk of being caught and punished, but she had to touch the garment of the true healer, the Lord Jesus Christ, who is compassionate and forgiving. Maybe she heard about the woman who was caught in the act of adultery whom the Lord Jesus set free with a warning. "Go now and leave your life of sin" (John 8:11).

She kept goading herself onward until she physically touched Him. By touching His garment, she would be connected to the divine power that could heal her from twelve long years of suffering. She would be delivered from bleeding, from the fear of public disgrace and shame; she would be whole again with restored health, dignity, and resources. She would be rescued from the religious elite who had every right under the law to stone her if they knew that she was bleeding in a public gathering.

She kept talking to herself, reflecting on everything she had gone through over the years. This bolstered her faith, which connected her to the power of God for healing and lasting deliverance. She *heard* about the healing power and grace that was upon the Lord. She *believed* what she heard. She *took a step of faith* by coming into the middle of the crowd to the Healer. She *touched* His garment by faith, despite all the obstacles. She was *healed*. She *knew* she was healed. She *testified* of the instant healing power of the Lord. Hence, her determination gave her courage to face all the challenges and to risk her life to receive from the Lord what no one else could give her. She knew the risk, the price, and the reward of being free.

Maybe she approached Him from behind so that the religious people would not stone her before she could touch His garment. Healing wasn't found in touching the Lord's garment, but in her faith in Him. Touching the garment was the expression of her full trust in His power. The Lord said, "Who touched My clothes?" When you touch Him by faith, you also will experience His power and testify to His goodness. Her touch of His garment was a physical expression of the desire of her heart to come closer, to experience His healing power.

As soon as she touched His garment, His power was released! Mark used the word "immediately" in describing the situation. "Immediately her bleeding stopped and she felt in her body that she was freed from her suffering" (Mark 5:29). This same healing power is available to you and me today! How is this possible?

First, the Word says she was healed immediately, straightaway, instantly, forthwith, as soon as she touched His garment. That means when the Lord finds individuals who reach out to Him by faith, God's response is without delay. There is no time gap.

Second, God demonstrates His power as an answer to the prayer of the believer. This woman experienced the power of healing in her body even before the flow of blood stopped because of her faith.

Third, when we touch His garment, He also touches us with the healing power that makes us whole instantly. That is what happened to the woman. At the same time that she touched Him, she received the power that flowed out from Him—and her blood flow stopped. She knew that she had been healed. She didn't go back to the doctors under whom she had suffered for many years. She received her heavenly certificate of healing and freedom from the Lord.

Fourth, the Lord asked who touched Him. The hands of the woman with the blood issue touched His garment, but her faith touched His power. "For she kept saying, If I only touch His garments, I shall be restored to health" (Mark 5:28 AMPC). The reason that Jesus asked the question that He did was because He felt His healing power leave Him.

Jesus' final words were the words of eternal freedom. "Daughter . . . Go in peace and be freed from your suffering" (Mark 5:34). For the woman who had experienced over a decade of horrific suffering and isolation, there was no greater reward than these words. She was free from the past's shame, from today's pain, and from tomorrow's fear and anxiety.

When you touch Him by faith, you will experience His power and be able to testify to His goodness. Have you ever touched Him by faith? Have you pressed into the difficulties through the crowds with great determination, reminding yourself of the truth that He can heal? It is not just about finding an answer or a solution to your problems; it is about glorifying Him through your faith and trust. When you do that, you will know His touch, and He will say to you, *Go in peace—security, safety, prosperity, felicity, and rest!*

Have you touched Him by faith—refusing all the hindrances with great determination?

Have you received from Him what only He can give?

Have you ever felt the freedom that comes from a supernatural experience or miracle?

Can you describe what you felt?

TWELVE

What Do You Want Me to Do for You?

"What do you want me to do for you?" Jesus asked him. The blind man said, "Rabbi, I want to see." "Go," said Jesus, "your faith has healed you." Immediately he received his sight and followed Jesus along the road.

Mark 10:51–52

This is an amazing story of determination, hope, foresight, of God redeeming time, of having a new identity established, of changing location, of becoming a disciple of the Lord Jesus, and so much more.

According to Mark's gospel account, this was the final journey of the Lord Jesus before His death. He was going to Jerusalem to celebrate the Passover festival, knowing He would then go to the cross to fulfill the prophecy of the Passover Lamb. I can only imagine what was going through His mind as He trudged the long journey to the place where He would soon be executed. He was so focused on His mission that His disciples were surprised not only by His focus but also by His pace along this journey. Mark recounts the Lord saying,

> "We are going up to Jerusalem," he said, "and the Son of Man will be delivered over to the chief priests and teachers of the law. They will condemn him to death and will hand him over to the Gentiles, who will mock him and spit on him, flog him and kill him. Three days later he will rise."
>
> Mark 10:33–34

This was a heavy journey.

As He was passing through the city of Jericho, He encountered Bartimaeus, a blind man, who was sitting by the roadside begging for money. When Bartimaeus heard the crowds clamoring to see Jesus, he asked what was going on. They told him that Jesus of Nazareth was passing by.

The blind beggar got up and took a few faltering steps toward the source of the noise. Because of his faith, he didn't waste any time in positioning himself for a lasting solution to his lifelong problems. As he physically positioned himself to encounter Jesus, he also positioned himself mentally, emotionally, and spiritually. When he sensed the unusual noise and commotion, he believed that this was the day for his sight to be recovered. When the crowd was loud, he increased his volume and shouted all the more. He refused to give up on an opportunity of a lifetime. He knew the time, and he redeemed it.

When you examine the few steps this blind man took for his lasting recovery, his actions were simple, but they were also very challenging. He believed what he heard; it was as simple as that. Not only did he believe, but he knew the prophecies, so he knew he was encountering the Messiah. The ability to open the eyes of the blind was meant to be a sign of the promised Messiah. You may notice that this miracle doesn't appear in the Old Testament. Isaiah states that the Messiah would come "to open eyes that are blind, to free captives from prison and to release from the dungeon those who sit in darkness" (Isaiah 42:7). King David also said, "The Lord gives sight to the blind, the Lord lifts up those who are bowed down, the Lord loves the righteous" (Psalm 146:8).

Bartimaeus believed this Jesus was the Messiah, and He was passing by him. He must have thought, "If I cry for mercy, He will heal me." Even though he was physically blind, his spiritual eyes were open. He was able to envision his future because of the mercy of the Messiah. What great faith!

This man was burdened by multiple problems that included his false identity as a blind outcast, social shame, cultural challenges, spiritual isolation, economic need, and physical limitations. His Messiah was passing by, so, "When he heard that it was Jesus of Nazareth, he began to shout" (Mark 10:47). He didn't waste a minute. He started right away, shouting to the Lord Jesus, saying, "Have mercy on me."

He didn't try to explain his condition, his family history, or the reason for his blindness. He believed that all would be covered under the mercy of the Messiah, the coming King, and the good Shepherd. By saying, "Jesus, Son of David," he declared what the experts of the law rejected publicly. His cry for mercy indicated that he went beyond just physical healing in appealing to the core of the expression of the love of God. He knew that no one could give that kind of mercy and love except the God of covenant.

Jesus heard His name and stopped, His focus and urgency to reach Jerusalem halted in this dramatic encounter. Jesus turned to His disciples and said, "Call him." The disciples went to Bartimaeus and said, "Cheer up! On your feet! He's calling you" (Mark 10:49). When the blind man heard that the Lord had stopped and was waiting for him, he responded in a very unusual manner. First, he threw away his cloak, which was, in many ways, his lifeline. It was his shelter from the elements, his security, and his covering. He cast it off like the past for the sake of his future. Then, he jumped to his feet without waiting for anybody to lead him. He came straight to the Lord without a guide. Then the Lord asked him this question, "What do you want me to do for you?" (verse 51).

Jesus was asking that question as a way of restoring Bartimaeus' dignity, even before He opened his eyes. Most likely this was the first time the man had been given an opportunity to make a request and be served. His answer was simple and easy, because it came crying out of the deepest desire of his heart: "I want to see."

The manifestation took place immediately, and his sight was restored. After he saw the Lord, it didn't take him any time to decide to follow Jesus. For him, following the Son of David was the greatest freedom. The beauty of this story was not just about the blind man's suffering, but also his refusal to give up. He continued to hope for a better future because of his faith. He believed that the Lord Jesus was the Messiah, he knew the prophecies of old, and he wouldn't let this chance pass him by.

This man threw away the past when he let go of his cloak and took a huge step toward victory. You have full permission to do the same. To everyone who cries out to the Lord for His mercy, His question is the same today and tomorrow: *What do you want Me to do for you?* In that question is restoration of dignity and identity. It comes with removing shame, breaking the curse, becoming a highly valued child of God, and changing your garment from darkness to light.

Furthermore, just as Bartimaeus moved from the kingdom of darkness to the Kingdom of light to see and follow the Lord, you can also if you are willing to answer the question of what you want Him to do for you. Once we answer that question, we live a life of testifying what He has done for us.

If Jesus asked you, "What do you want Me to do for you?" how would you answer His question?

Do you have faith to believe He not only can do what you're asking but will do it?

Could you or have you let go of your past and stepped out in faith to receive from the Lord?

Have you received the freedom only He can provide in any area of your life?

THIRTEEN

Friends, Haven't You Any Fish?

> Early in the morning, Jesus stood on the shore, but the disciples did not realize that it was Jesus. He called out to them, "Friends, haven't you any fish?" "No," they answered.
>
> *John 21:4–5*

Three years before the death of Jesus, the disciples began their walk with Him by giving up their fishing profession. One day, the Lord Jesus came to the shore where the men were fishing. He negotiated with Simon (later known as Peter) to borrow his boat as a place for Him to teach that morning. After He had finished teaching, He said to Simon, "Put out into deep water, and let down the nets for a catch" (Luke 5:4).

Simon Peter said, "Master, we have toiled all night and caught nothing; nevertheless at *Your word I will let down the net*" (Luke 5:5 NKJV, emphasis added). I love the phrase *at Your word*. There is a creative power in the word of the Lord. He created the world by the power of His word. "'Let there be light,' and there was light"

(Genesis 1:3). All things are still sustained by His powerful word. There is miracle-working power in His word, if we just believe and obey.

Simon Peter obeyed the word of Jesus and experienced his first miracle. He and his fellow fishermen caught so many fish they had to ask other men to come and help them, and they quickly filled both boats. This miracle took place because of their obedience to do what the Lord had told them to do.

The disciples also witnessed the miracle at the wedding in Cana of Galilee. They were with Jesus at that wedding, and Jesus' mother, Mary, came to her Son and told Him that the wedding hosts had run out of wine. This was an absolute disaster for the hosts that could have resulted in terrible social shame. Knowing this, Mary didn't ask Jesus for His help or tell Him to do anything. She just relayed the problem. Then, she turned around and told the attendants, "Do whatever he tells you" (John 2:5). In obedience to the word of the Lord Jesus, they filled the empty ceremonial washing jars to the brim with water. When they came back and told Him they had filled them, "Then he told them, 'Now draw some out and take it to the master of the banquet'" (John 2:8).

The master tasted it and witnessed the miracle of water changing to wine. The only puzzling thing for the master of the ceremony was why they had kept the best wine until the end. The answer was that they didn't have it until the Lord stepped in and changed tasteless water into the best wine, colorless water into colorful wine, water without smell or fragrance into wine of great aroma! Simon Peter, along with the other disciples, was an eyewitness to this first miracle of transition from the Old Testament promises to the New Testament reality. The glory of God had been revealed, according to what was promised, and those who were at the wedding saw it. "And the glory of the LORD will be revealed, and all people will see it together. For the mouth of the LORD has spoken" (Isaiah 40:5).

When Simon Peter threw out his net at Jesus' command and caught a shocking haul of fish, his life changed completely. His calling was not to catch fish. The Lord spoke to him and revealed, "'Don't be afraid; from now on you will fish for people.' So they pulled their boats up on shore, left everything and followed him" (Luke 5:10–11).

This was the start of their journey, forsaking everything and following the Lord in obedience to His word. They followed Him and were taken through the journey of a lifetime. For these disciples, the first three and a half years of their walk were spent with the Lord. The remainder of their years on earth and in ministry was spent with the Holy Spirit.

The first step to being made fishers of men was gaining the right understanding of spiritual authority. The disciples faced this early during their journey when the Lord sent them out with power and authority. "The seventy-two returned with joy and said, 'Lord, even the demons submit to us in your name'" (Luke 10:17). The Lord used that experience to help the disciples refocus their relationship with Him as the giver and source of all power and authority, instead of building their ministry on that one-time victory. He said,

> I have given you authority to trample on snakes and scorpions and to overcome all the power of the enemy; nothing will harm you. However, do not rejoice that the spirits submit to you, *but rejoice that your names are written in heaven.*
>
> Luke 10:19–20, emphasis added

The second step for the disciples was learning to deal with fear and doubt in order to be equipped followers of Jesus, ready to fulfill His purpose on earth. On their journey, the disciples faced fear and doubt many times, even when the Lord was physically with them. They were afraid when the storm came and the waves swept over their boat, but the Lord and Master of all was sleeping in the boat (see Matthew 8:24). They were terrified when they saw Him walking on the water (see Matthew 14:25–26). They were afraid of those who might harm them (see John 20:19). They were afraid when He was taken to the cross. Fear was the main reason Peter denied the Lord three times and the others scattered and left Him (see Luke 22:54–62).

In the process of making His disciples fishers of men, the Lord helped them overcome fear and doubt by placing in them a spirit of courage and a clearer perspective about His presence. This spirit lives in you today and can empower you to protect your joy and enhance your spirit with boldness so that you can walk with an attitude or a mindset of being an overcomer like the Lord Jesus.

> Fixing our eyes on Jesus, the pioneer and perfecter of faith. For the joy set before him he endured the cross, scorning its shame, and sat down at the right hand of the throne of God.
>
> Hebrews 12:2

After the resurrection, Jesus revealed Himself to the disciples for the third time. "Afterward Jesus appeared again to his disciples, by the Sea of Galilee" (John 21:1). The key phrase is, Jesus revealed Himself to the disciples again. He started with them at the seaside while they were fishing. When they went without catching anything, He performed a miracle, filling their boats with fish. After the miracle, He revealed to them His plan for their lives—which was their prophetic destiny—by declaring, "I will make you fishers of men." They accepted that promise without fully understanding what it would take to be fishers of men.

Jesus' death had created not only doubt and fear but also hopelessness. Even after they saw Him twice as the risen Lord, they still decided to go back to their old profession of fishing by following Simon Peter. "'I'm going out to fish,' Simon Peter told them, and they said, 'We'll go with you'" (John 21:3). None of them asked, "What about the call and the promise of the Lord?" They picked up their old fishing nets they had left behind for more than three years and went back to fishing.

They tried fishing all night using their past experiences and professional skills without any success. That was their situation when the Lord met them at the shore. It seems they had forgotten what He had told them the first time: "Follow Me, and I will make you fishers of men" (Matthew 4:19 NKJV). Jesus kept His promise and came back. This time it was not to call them, but to reveal Himself to them again. That revelation transformed their lives once and for all.

This time, He waited for them at the shore until they came back from an unsuccessful fishing trip at daybreak. When they came close to the shore, He asked, "Friends, haven't you any fish?" In other words, "Did you produce any result by going back to what I told you to let go of and follow Me?" Their answer was simple and straightforward. "No." The Lord was hungry for the fruit of their obedience rather than their fish or bread. How do we know this? Because He had already prepared a breakfast for them before they came to the shore. The question He asked was to affirm that He had called them for Himself, and whatever they did should be for the glory of His name.

There is, however, one last question He would ask them. That fundamental question was not about fish or bread or even about their calling. It was about their love for Him. In order to entrust His future Church into their hands and to have them represent Him in His absence, He wanted to know the level and depth of their love for Him. He asked Peter three times, "Do you love me?" (see John 21:15–17). "Do you love me more than these?" This last phrase, "more than these," was different. Loving Him more than everything in our lives is the foundation of our being and ministry. After the Lord heard Peter's answer, He moved from questions to a command: "Follow Me!" This was a part of their final commissioning for ministry and for life.

To be able to answer "Do you truly love me more than these?" leads to a life of commitment to follow Him—whatever the cost might be. The Lord started by asking them to follow Him and finished by asking them to follow Him. If you are a follower of the Lord, you should have the fruit of obedience as an expression of your love for Him, and you should walk with determination to live for Him.

Questions of Miracles

How would you answer the question "Do you love Me?"

_____
_____
_____

"Do you love Me more than these?"

_____
_____
_____

How are you following Him?

_____
_____
_____

Have you faced fear and doubt in your walk with the Lord? Did He help you remove it?

_____
_____
_____

FOURTEEN

What Shall I Give You?

> On that night God appeared to Solomon, and said to him,
> "Ask! What shall I give you?"
>
> 2 *Chronicles* 1:7 NKJV

Can you imagine someone coming to you and saying that you could ask for whatever you wanted with complete assurance that you would receive it? It might sound like something from a fairy tale, but it happened in the Bible. This is what happened to the young King Solomon after he was inaugurated as the king of Israel.

Before we talk about Solomon, we need to start with his father. King David had been anointed by God Himself, and the Lord was with him (see Psalm 89:20). David was successful in every mission he undertook, whether it be on the battlefield or politically (see 1 Samuel 18:14). He was a worshiper of the one true God and an anointed and skillful musician (see 1 Samuel 16:18). He was a brave warrior and a well-spoken, fine-looking man (see 1 Samuel 16:18). He had a passionate zeal for the Lord, he was a man after God's own heart (see Acts 13:22), and he sought to do God's will out of a deep love and reverence (see Acts 13:36).

David was anointed by God to make history and to establish a godly standard in the kingdom by modeling a God-fearing life. He was to shepherd the people of God with a lasting covenant. He was chosen and anointed, but not because of his giftings, his experiences, or his education. He was selected because of his heart for God, and God loved David deeply. "I will not take my love from him, nor will I ever betray my faithfulness" (Psalm 89:33).

David started by correcting history immediately after he was anointed as king, even before he sat on the throne. There had been many atrocities and blasphemies committed by other kings of Israel, and David knew he had to make amends. He corrected history by killing the giant who came to enslave the people of Israel. He restored victory in the name of the Lord. David's anointing was for true authority and victory over the enemy. "The enemy will not get the better of him; the wicked will not oppress him" (Psalm 89:22).

Through David's anointing, God broke the cycle of Israel's sinful patterns and desires and established His plans for the nation. He simultaneously led David to destroy the enemies of the people of God in glorious military victories. David's anointing was a sign of God's faithfulness to him and Israel. David also broke the cycle of jealousy that was rooted in the throne room of Israel between Saul and David. Instead, he ushered in the spirit of a brotherly covenant among the generations.

David's godly example brought back a national spirit, desiring to seek after the Lord and His presence. This is important because the thing that makes the presence of God stay among the people is not the skill of a king or leader, it's the heart of the worshipers. You can only keep the manifested presence of God through pure hearts and holy reverence for God. The good news is that God promises to give you a new, pure heart so that you can see Him and worship Him.

Throughout his life, David's desire was to be in the presence of the Lord. You can read about this throughout the book of Psalms.

Many times, he cried out to be in the house of the Lord and dwell in His presence. The Lord was with David, and His presence gave him success, strength, and peace. In order for there to be restoration for the Body of Christ, you and I need to cultivate a true desire for His presence more than anything else and cry out for the full manifestation of His glory.

David's desire for the presence of the God of his fathers motivated him, causing him to seek God more than anything else. He was a man of prayer who purposely determined that he would regularly cry out to the Lord, wherever he was or through whatever was going on in his life. Across his lifetime, David sought to be with the Lord more than he sought to become the king of Israel. God wants His children to seek Him and call upon His mighty name by the Holy Spirit above all other desires.

What does this have to do with King Solomon? David's relationship with the Lord opened the door for Solomon's relationship with God. Because of their relationship, the Lord promised David a son who would sit on his throne: Solomon. This was an overwhelming responsibility for a young Solomon. In God's kindness, He revealed Himself to Solomon in Solomon's dreams after he was anointed king of Israel. In these dreams, the Lord asked him, "What shall I give you?"

Solomon is the only king who was given a blank check to write whatever amount he desired. I believe the reason for such generosity and abundance was because of the relationship God had with David and the promises and blessings that came from that relationship. King Solomon referred to this when he said, "Praise be to the LORD, the God of Israel, who with his own hand has fulfilled what he promised with his own mouth to my father David" (1 Kings 8:15).

When the Lord asked young Solomon what the desire of his heart was, this was his reply.

> You have shown great kindness to your servant, my father David, because he was faithful to you and righteous and upright in heart.

> You have continued this great kindness to him and have given him a son to sit on his throne this very day. Now, Lord my God, you have made your servant king in place of my father David. But I am only a little child and do not know how to carry out my duties. Your servant is here among the people you have chosen, a great people, too numerous to count or number. So give your servant a discerning heart to govern your people and to distinguish between right and wrong. For who is able to govern this great people of yours?
>
> 1 Kings 3:6–9

Solomon's answer pleased the Lord very much because it reflected a sincere heart. As a result, God made him wise, gave him a discerning heart, and blessed him with honor and riches above any other king. Solomon started with the great inheritance he received from the Lord because of the faithfulness and the righteousness of David. He asked for wisdom and a discerning heart (insight and understanding) to continue stewarding God's favor toward His people. He admitted his personal inadequacy by saying that he was just a child, and he did not know how to carry out his duties of being a king over this great people of God. He understood the responsibility of leading the people of covenant, God's people.

God responded to Solomon's request by depositing godly wisdom into his spirit. When you walk with God with a pure heart and sincere faith and do His will on earth, He doesn't only give you the desires of your heart, but He also blesses you with His generosity. He is able to do more than what you can even ask or imagine.

What would you like to ask God to give you?

_____

_____

_____

Is your request from a pure heart? Does it benefit you or others?

Do you have a heart for worship like David did? Do you have a true desire not only to come into God's presence but to be able to remain in His presence?

PART THREE

QUESTIONS OF CHARACTER

In this section, we will address key issues pertaining to a person's character. We will also learn how maturity is forged through obedience to God and exercising faith in the Spirit of God.

FIFTEEN

Where Are My Honor and Reverence?

> A son honors his father,
> And a servant his master.
> If then I am the Father,
> Where is My honor?
> And if I am a Master,
> Where is My reverence?
> Says the Lord of hosts
> To you priests who despise My name.
> Yet you say, "In what way have we despised Your name?"
>
> *Malachi 1:6 NKJV*

The above verse describes a time in Israel's history when the people of God had lost all their passion for the Lord. They had completely abandoned the fire of true worship. So the Lord asked the people of His covenant two interrelated questions: *If I am the Father, where is My honor? And if I am a Master, where is My reverence?*

At this time, the people of God continued to call Him Father without honoring Him as a father. They referred to him as their Lord or King, but they didn't walk in fear and reverence of the Lord of Hosts. They disrespected the name of the Lord by their actions when they brought imperfect sacrifices and placed them on the holy altar of God—they brought blind, crippled, and diseased animals for a sacrifice when the Lord required spotless sacrifices.

How did this happen? It began when the Israelites started doubting God's love. This led them to stop honoring Him as a father, and once they lost the father-child relationship, they didn't care about His Lordship. They didn't fear or obey Him. That led them to a place of rebelling against God, not only defiling the sacrifice of worship but also becoming bold in declaring that it was useless to serve God. They were given a warning not to be negligent in serving God, but they didn't take this warning to heart. Instead, they despised serving the Lord.

God expressed His great disapproval toward this blatant lack of respect, as it appeared not only in the kind of offerings they brought but also through their words and actions. They disrespected the word of the Lord and dishonored Him willfully by turning away from His commands. The religious leaders were called to teach the people of God to fear and honor His name among the nations, but when they turned away from the Lord's commands, they caused many to stumble and violate the covenant. This was just another form of defilement.

The people broke their covenant with God by not honoring Him, they broke their covenants with one another, and they broke their marriage covenants. The Lord had instructed them not to mix in marriage with idol worshipers, which would turn their hearts to false gods, but they didn't obey (see Malachi 2:11).

They robbed God in their giving. "You are under a curse—your whole nation—because you are robbing me" (Malachi 3:9). The Lord's plan for His people had been always to bless them; however, this blessing required that His people follow divine principles.

When we give, we honor God the Creator and Redeemer. Withholding what belongs to God is dishonoring the owner and giver of everything. As His child, you have received the good gift of life and provision from Him so that you can honor Him. You are given the opportunity to honor Him by giving back from what you have received in the form of tithes, firstfruits, and love offerings. God doesn't have financial needs, but His desire is for you to be blessed by honoring Him in your giving. This is why holding back in your giving is not only stopping your worship but also robbing God.

Because of all this dishonor, the Lord refused to hear the prayers of His people or accept their offerings. He promised, however, that if they returned to Him, He would return to them and open the windows of heaven over them (see Malachi 3:10). Then they wouldn't be called cursed by the Lord but blessed.

And it is here you will see that the Lord found a few individuals who set themselves apart. "Then those who feared the Lord talked with each other, and the Lord listened and heard. A scroll of remembrance was written in his presence concerning those who feared the Lord and honored his name" (Malachi 3:16).

These individuals began by restoring to Israel what was lost, the fear of the Lord. In other words, the fear of the Lord was what motivated them to come together and talk about the words, the character, and the ways of God. They recognized God as the Father of Israel and the Lord of their lives. As such, they sought out others who feared God in spite of what was going in their culture.

In every generation, the Lord finds people who are jealous for His glory even when they feel that they are alone or are a minority. Think of Elijah, who said to the Lord, "The Israelites have rejected your covenant, torn down your altars, and put your prophets to death with the sword. I am the only one left, and now they are trying to kill me too" (1 Kings 19:10). The Lord was pleased with his commitment to Him and assured him that he was not alone. "Yet I reserve seven thousand in Israel—all whose knees have not bowed down to Baal and all whose mouths have not kissed him" (1 Kings 19:18). It is very encouraging to know that when you stand for the cause of Christ, you may be a minority, but you're not alone.

Your responsibility, therefore, is to look for those the Lord has prepared and raised up for this hour to talk with, fellowship with, pray with, and serve the Lord with. Let's find those with whom we can resolve together to restore the fear and honor of the Lord in the unity of the Spirit, so that the Lord would declare over the Body of Christ:

1. Your prayers and concerns for the glory of My name are heard.
2. Your prayers and desires are recorded in My book, and you will receive the desires of your heart.
3. You will be Mine among your generation: "They're mine, all mine" (Malachi 3:17 MSG).
4. You will be used as My special or peculiar treasure.
5. You will be spared just as a father spares an obedient child on the day of judgment.
6. You will see the distinction between the righteous and the wicked, between those who serve God and those who do not (see Malachi 3:18).
7. You, who revere My name, the sun of righteousness will rise with healing in its wings for you on the day of judgment (see Malachi 4:2).
8. You will be free to walk in victory, and you shall tread down the lawless and wicked (see Malachi 4:3).
9. You will have power to turn the hearts of the fathers to their children and the hearts of the children to the fathers and the hearts of Israel to the Lord (see Malachi 4:6).
10. You will be used to restore the covenant for the purifying fire for acceptable worship. "Then the LORD will have men

who will bring offerings in righteousness, and the offerings of Judah and Jerusalem will be acceptable to the LORD, as in days gone by, as in former years" (Malachi 3:3–4).

These are some of the blessings that come when we set about restoring the Lord's honor for the glory and praise of His name. This is the only way to bring back the fire of worship that is acceptable for the Lord to come back to His temple. "'Then suddenly the LORD you are seeking will come to his temple; the messenger of the covenant, whom you desire, will come,' says the LORD Almighty" (Malachi 3:1). It was a preparation process for the fullness of the glory that was declared by John the Baptist, which was fulfilled by the Lord Jesus Christ. "But after me comes one who is more powerful than I, whose sandals I am not worthy to carry. He will baptize you with the Holy Spirit and fire" (Matthew 3:11).

We should focus on becoming an instrument in answer to the Lord's prayer if we want to see the glory of the Lord in the middle of a society that has turned its back on the Lord. If we want to see the churches who have become lukewarm by neglecting true worship and losing their first love turn around to take pride and boast in Him, we should set about restoring His honor on the earth. We will see people unified by becoming those who live to honor and exalt His holy name. Only then will we be empowered to restore His glory, be inspired to host His presence, and be anointed to declare the Gospel of the Kingdom among the nations.

Are you honoring God in your giving?

Are you honoring God in your love walk?

Are you being obedient in serving God as He has called you?

Do you truly know Him as Father?

While reading this, did the Holy Spirit convict you to repent of something so that you can restore His place of honor as your Father?

SIXTEEN

Where Are You Going?

> And he said, "Hagar, slave of Sarai, where have you come from, and where are you going?" "I'm running away from my mistress Sarai," she answered. Then the angel of the LORD told her, "Go back to your mistress and submit to her."
>
> *Genesis 16:8–9*

Before you determine your goals or your destination, it is necessary to know where you have come from. Not only is your starting point a foundation, but it is your history that creates your values and the basis for your future vision. Knowing the journey you have been on does not mean you need to accept everything as it is, but without that knowledge, you cannot evaluate your past or learn how to correct your mistakes. When you do that, you will be able to build something that will last for the future.

You can do this by answering three simple yet practical questions: Where was I? Where am I? Where am I going? When you ask these questions, you must ask them through the lenses of faith, hope, and love. The Bible says, "And now these three remain: faith, hope and love. But the greatest of these is love"

(1 Corinthians 13:13). Faith, hope, and love are the three reigning virtues that help you evaluate the foundation of your life in the past and help you build a strong foundation for the future.

Faith helps you define what you believe, and it affirms your identity and goals in life. By faith, you can take action to please and honor God. Faith gives you the strength to dream about tomorrow with greater hope. By faith, you overcome the challenges of the past, which include your setbacks, challenges, and strongholds that have affected not only your past but your future. You can restore the foundation of your life by faith in obedience to the Word of the Lord in order to answer God's question of "Where have you come from?"

You move forward by correcting the past for the sake of your future. Please note that the past is not your home, so it is not necessary to dwell there—simply correct it. Hope creates an expectancy to live a life that is worthy of the glory of God by acting upon what you believe. It also enables you to dream about the future without fear or guilt. Hope creates an anticipation and excitement that renews your joy and strengthens you. Thus, by faith you please God, and with hope you take steps of obedience in accordance with His will to honor Him.

You express your love for Him by daily obeying His revealed will for your life. Love is the essence of the life we live for God and others. Together faith, hope, and love provide the foundation for answering these three essential questions of life as we evaluate our progress on our walk. Where was I? Where am I? Where am I going?

These are the questions Hagar faced when she ran away from Abraham and Sarah's home. The Lord promised Abraham that He would bless him, give him offspring, and make him into a great nation. Abraham had left his family and his country to obediently follow God. There are always blessings that follow obedience. This elderly couple waited 25 years for God to fulfill His promise to provide them a son.

During that waiting period, however, Sarah became antsy. She convinced herself that she and her husband needed to take matters into their own hands. They had already waited ten years to receive the promise. Little did she know she would have to wait over twenty years to see the fulfillment of God's promise. But for now, all she saw was that the promise wasn't materializing. Maybe she felt that she and her husband were running out of time; maybe she was sick of hoping and waiting. Sarah came up with a suggestion that would give Abraham his promised son, and Abraham agreed to it.

Abraham took Hagar, his Egyptian slave, as a wife and had a child with her. This man of faith and a friend of God didn't ask the Lord about this plan—even once. He took Hagar to be his wife, and she conceived. To human eyes, it would look like the promise was fulfilled; however, this was not God's fulfillment. It was man's attempt at bringing something to pass.

Rapid promotion can make a person either very humble and grateful or very prideful. The latter is what happened to Hagar. She felt indispensable. She forgot where she came from. The minute she felt that she was secure as Abraham's wife, a man who was chosen to become the channel of the fulfillment of the promises of God, Hagar rejected all accountability and began to refuse to submit. Hagar began to despise Sarah; she felt she was not a slave any longer because she had given her master a son. She didn't bother to express gratitude to Sarah for the opportunity she had been given or her radical change in circumstances. Because of her posture, the Bible says, "Then Sarai mistreated Hagar; so she fled from her" (Genesis 16:6). Hagar was trapped in this deception, and the circumstances of her home life became miserable. She left Abraham's home to become a wanderer in the wilderness.

Once a person leaves his or her position because of pride and deception, there is a price to pay. In the Garden of Eden, the Lord shut the gate because Adam and Eve left their place of fellowship with Him (see Genesis 3:24). The Lord told Isaac to stay where he was during a great famine (see Genesis 26). He told him not to go to Egypt to look for food and that if he stayed where he was, God would bless him. Isaac obeyed and was blessed a hundredfold during the famine time. The question of "Where did you come from?" asks why you left your position. God blesses us in the place where He places us for His purpose.

Hagar left her place and was found in the desert beside the road to Shur. The word *shur* means "wall." Hagar faced not only the desert but a wall she could not pass over. That means she was stopped in the desert without any hope. "The angel of the LORD found Hagar near a spring in the desert; it was the spring that is beside the road to *Shur*" (Genesis 16:7, emphasis added). She had left a place of honor for the desert, which was a place of punishment. The angel asked her, "Hagar, slave of Sarai, where have you come from, and where are you going?" (verse 8).

God's first question for Hagar in the wilderness of wandering was *Where did you come from?* This is God's question for all who neglect or despise His opportunities. This question is about your mindset and heart attitude. Your attitude and the condition of your heart enable you to make necessary adjustments through repentance so that your vision will not be aborted because of pride.

These are the most important questions to answer to correct the past and to shape the future. Once Hagar answered the questions, the Lord's command was straightforward. She was to go back and submit so that she could correct the past through repentance. With obedience to that command from the Lord, she would receive the promises of God that were released over her future. She was given the assurance of being heard and seen by God as He revealed Himself to her. What a beautiful picture of receiving restoration of the past with the hope of a brighter future! You can have the same results when you are willing to repent and submit to His plan.

Where Are You Going?

If God asked you, "Where did you come from?" could you answer Him?

Do you know where you are going?

Have you let pride dictate your future to you?

What is the condition or attitude of your heart?

SEVENTEEN

What Is This Sound I Hear?

> Listen! Obedience is better than sacrifice, and submission
> is better than offering the fat of rams.
>
> 1 Samuel 15:22 NLT

Achieving success is much more than your accomplishments, your possessions, or crossing self-directed goals off your list. Success in God's estimation has everything to do with wholehearted obedience to His will.

God delivered His people, who were under the headship of Moses, from Egyptian bondage after they had spent more than four hundred years in slavery. When they came out of bondage, they rebelled. As a result of that rebellion, they wandered in the desert for an additional forty years. The majority of the original freed slaves eventually died in the wilderness. An entire generation had to die in the desert because of rebellion—it's a tragedy. Joshua, Caleb, and many of the Israelite children who were born during the nation's wandering remained (see Numbers 14:20–38).

After Moses' death, Joshua led the remaining company of people who served the Lord. Following Joshua's death and the death of the elders who supported him, however, there arose another generation who did not acknowledge the Lord or the works He had done for Israel. Because of this, they ended up serving idols and abandoned the Lord.

God saw Israel's need for righteous leadership, so He raised up judges and prophets to deliver and govern them. The people, however, refused to listen to these God-appointed men (see Judges 21:25). One of God's appointed leaders at that time was a man by the name of Samuel, an anointed prophet, judge, and priest who was destined by God to do according to what was in His mind (see 1 Samuel 2:35). He walked faithfully with God and became a great leader.

Yet Israel was still spiritually blind. The nation's elders asked Samuel to appoint a human king for them. What Israel failed to realize was they already had a king over them. The one true King. In response, even though His heart was grieved by their request, God granted them a king in Saul. King Saul was anointed to lead Israel under God's guidance and instruction, which would come by way of his close collaboration with Samuel the prophet. It was God's design that together they would faithfully carry out His will and purpose for His people.

When Samuel delivered the word of the Lord and anointed Saul, he was very specific in his description of the ways God would confirm this new call on Saul's life. God changed him into another man by changing his heart (see 1 Samuel 10:6). After Samuel's official declaration of Saul as king, the Spirit of the Lord came upon Saul with power, and from that time forward began to work through him to deliver God's people from their enemies. Saul's story takes many different turns, because even though he began as a man who carried the Lord's authority to rule, he was not fully obedient.

A crucial truth must be grasped from this story about Saul: *Partial obedience is actually total disobedience!* Obedience is the hallmark of humility, while disobedience reeks of pride and arrogance. Soon after Saul's anointing ceremony, a group of Philistines assembled to fight Israel. Saul wanted to offer a sacrifice to the

Lord and seek His will in the matter, but Samuel instructed him to wait until he could arrive. Saul was not to perform the sacrifice as he wasn't a priest; however, when Saul saw that enemy forces were closing in and that his military was scattering, he panicked and made the sacrifice (see 1 Samuel 13:7–14).

Rest assured, your character and your obedience will be tested in moments like these when you are under stress and it feels as though everything is on the line. You will have many opportunities to choose to either move out on your own, as Saul did, or wait on God. Saul failed to follow Samuel's charge, and as a result, he failed to pass a crucial character test.

When Samuel arrived, he asked, "What have you done?" He was really asking, "How did you become so foolish?" The fear of the Lord is wisdom in its purest sense. When a person walks in the fear of God, he or she will find it is not as difficult to wait upon His timing.

Anxiety and fear are two of the most common means employed by the enemy to provoke God's people to move outside of His timing. King Saul ended up losing his kingdom because he did not wait on the Lord's timing. Instead, he operated in disobedience. When we fail to recognize and adhere to God's timing, we miss our *kairos*. We miss watching Him uniquely orchestrate circumstances to converge under His providence. Redeeming time is all about maximizing opportunities through discerning time correctly. Maximized opportunities are the fruit of wisdom.

Again, I stress this fact: Your character is most often tested in the area of obedience to the known will of God. When people reject their higher authority, they create a root of pride that comes from that disobedience. Saul chose to deny the authority of Samuel, the one God placed over him, by doing his own thing instead of waiting for the high priest. At times, you might find it easy to justify your disobedience, but no matter how you slice it—disobedience is disobedience.

In another instance, the Lord gave Saul a specific assignment: destroy the Amalekites (see 1 Samuel 15:3). The Amalekites were the first nation to oppose the Israelites' entry into their Promised Land. They refused to let God's people pass through their land and fought against them in an attempt to push the nation back into slavery in Egypt. By doing this, they opposed God's will for His chosen people.

Because of the Amalekites' resistance, the Lord instructed the Israelites through Moses to someday eliminate the Amalekites (see Deuteronomy 25:19). Centuries later, Saul was called upon to execute this sentence, but he only partially obeyed. He might as well have ignored the Lord's command completely. The complete story, which is well worth reading, is found in 1 Samuel 15.

Saul was given the mandate to attack the Amalekites and totally destroy everything that belonged to them, but Saul and his army spared the Amalekite king, Agag, and the best of the sheep and cattle, the fat calves, and the lambs. They destroyed what they thought was worthless, and they kept what they deemed valuable. When Saul opted for partial obedience, he grieved the Lord. As a result of his action, Saul ended up turning away from God. This brings me to my next point.

Partial or selective obedience is not only disobedience but turning against God. Turning away from God means denying His power and authority. When your heart turns away from God and personal significance becomes more important than God's purpose and glory, you deceive yourself and become an idolater of self.

Spirituality is not measured by your overt religious activity, but by the purity of your heart, which is demonstrated through a life of obedience. You must always guard your heart and be consistent in your integrity. Being willing to sacrifice is important to the Lord, but He never asks you to do so at the expense of obedience. "To obey is better than sacrifice" (1 Samuel 15:22). People's needs are important, but it's best to serve their truest needs as you endeavor to hear and obey the Spirit of the living God.

Saul chose the fear of man over the fear of the Lord. May we learn well from his example and maintain a posture of wisdom in the fear of the Lord, keeping the main thing the main thing.

Humility is forged in the fires of testing that come through obedience to the Lord. Let our hearts desire nothing less than complete surrender to His good and perfect will and plan.

Has there been a time when you didn't obey God?

Did you just disobey or were you not open to His timing?

Did fear play a role in your decision to disobey?

Was the outcome of your decision worth it in the end?

EIGHTEEN

Who Are These Men with You?

> God came to Balaam and asked,
> "Who are these men with you?"
> *Numbers 22:9*

It was and is very typical for the prophets of God to seek His face and ask Him questions. In this case, however, God was the one asking the questions. He approached the prophet Balaam to ask about his relationship with strangers who came from the land of Moab.

Before we dive in, here is a little background. The name Balaam means "not of the people." Because he was a stranger among the Israelites, Balaam was more likely to accept strangers into his home. The strangers in question were sent by the king of Moab. Moabites were people who lived east of the Jordan River. Historically, they were the enemy of the Israelites. In addition, when they heard what the Lord had done for His people and how He had brought them out of Egypt, the Moabites were terrified. They knew the Lord was with His people, and He was fighting for them.

Balak, the king of Moab, realized that he could not defeat Israel in war, so he decided to send his officials to bribe the Lord's prophet to curse the people of God. The king's agenda was never a secret; it was stated plainly from the outset (see Numbers 22:5–6).

Throughout the Bible, the spirit of Moab represents the following:

An immoral beginning. The man named Moab was the son of Lot, and his mother was Lot's older daughter. Moab's immoral beginning later became a hindrance. It is very important to deal with the past for the sake of present peace and future hope. The grace of God is available to set anybody free who is in bondage to past failures.

The opposition of the enemy. The Moabites were among the people who were opposed to the people of God. They fought the Israelites time and again. Today, Moab represents anything the enemy uses to oppose and return us to our former years of bondage.

The source of a curse. The Moabites planned to bring a curse on the Israelites. Balaam tried to curse the Israelites, but God did not allow it to happen. This is a way that the enemy brings opposition, wages an ongoing war, or tries to bring a curse upon the people of God or those committed to fulfill God's purposes. But the enemy can't do anything as long as we're committed to God and following Him (see Deuteronomy 23:5).

A source of temptation. In Numbers 22–25, the Moabites couldn't bring a curse on the Israelites, so they came up with another tactic. Just before the Israelites crossed the Jordan River and entered the Promised Land, the Moabites brought judgment on them by enticing them into sexual immorality and idol worship. When the enemy cannot bring a curse on us and can't oppose us, he changes his tactics and deceitfully comes to bring the curse or judgment of God upon God's people.

A source of thievery. Later in Judges 3:12–30, the Moabites captured some Israelite territory when the Israelites came into the

Promised Land. After the Israelites settled, the Moabites didn't leave them alone. This is the work of the enemy. He doesn't stop harassing us once we enter our "promised land." He still wants to take God's blessings from us.

A threat to the king. The Moabites started threatening, and at times, fighting with the king of the Israelites. The Israelites established their kingdom, took the territory, and didn't rest, but continued to fight against this constant threat (see 1 Samuel 14:47 and 2 Samuel 8:2).

A drain on resources. The Moabites raided the Israelites. They used force to overcome God's people and refused to pay the Israelites what they had legally agreed to pay them (see 2 Kings 3).

This is who Balaam, the prophet of God, was entertaining in his home. The Lord made Balaam a prophet to bring His message and provide guidance that would ultimately bless Israel. Even though he knew his calling and the plan of the enemy, Balaam still welcomed the officials from Moab into his house with the invitation "Spend the night here." They presented their bribe, and Balaam promised to bring God's answer to their bribe back to them the next morning.

The Lord came that night to Balaam and asked him, "Who are these men with you?" God's question to Balaam was not about hospitality; it was about having the wrong association and alignment. Why was Balaam hosting the people who desired to destroy Israel?

God had to speak to Balaam to remind him that because Israel was blessed, Balaam must not curse them. Still, Balaam toyed with the idea of taking the bribe from Moab. He sent back the princes of Moab by saying that the Lord refused to let him go with them. Balaam was a leader with a gift, but without integrity or character.

King Balak tried to entice Balaam again by sending a higher-level official who was offering a better reward. Although Balaam knew the Lord had already said no to Moab, Balaam again offered hospitality to the officials Balak had sent. He encouraged the Moabites to stay with him overnight while he found out if the Lord would change His mind.

The Lord came back again that night. This time the Lord told Balaam to go with the Moabites, but the Lord was very angry with Balaam. God granted His permission because it was clear Balaam's heart simply wasn't right. This is what happens when you try to use prayer to justify your personal desire. That kind of prayer is a type of witchcraft, which goes against the revealed will of God.

Because of His anger, the Lord sent His angel to oppose Balaam on his way to Moab. The angel of the Lord waited for him on the road with a drawn sword in his hand to strike Balaam down. The strangest thing is that Balaam didn't even see the angel, but his donkey did.

Balaam was blinded spiritually because of his love of money and because of the deception of the enemy of God's people. When his donkey saw the sword of the Lord's angel, it turned into a field to avoid it. In response, Balaam beat the donkey in anger. The angel of the Lord stood in a narrow path, and the donkey pressed against the wall to avoid the drawn sword. Balaam beat it again because his foot was crushed between the donkey and the wall. Finally, the Lord opened the donkey's mouth, and the donkey and the angel spoke to Balaam. The Lord had already opened the eyes of Balaam's donkey; now He also opened the donkey's mouth. The animal rebuked Balaam for his abuse, and the angel of the Lord rebuked Balaam for his spiritual blindness (see Numbers 22–24).

The question we should ask is, Where did this start? Balaam began to go astray when he welcomed and hosted the enemy's messengers that first time. Balaam rushed to gain profit, and that led him to error. The Lord's visit and question were meant to stop him and rescue him, but Balaam didn't obey the Lord's command.

Our downfall begins when we dwell on the thoughts or desires that the enemy sends. Whatever we are willing to welcome in against the will of God is what destroys our vision and anointing.

The other warning we can heed from Balaam's life is that once the enemy finds an access point, he doesn't easily give up. The enemy's plan is to bring God's judgment against His people and to disqualify anyone who is anointed.

Balaam lost his role as a prophet and became a teacher of evil. "There are some among you who hold to the teaching of Balaam, who taught Balak to entice the Israelites to sin so that they ate food sacrificed to idols and committed sexual immorality" (Revelation 2:14). Balaam's story demonstrates how wrong associations and love for what is evil can result in us being blinded to God's purpose. Welcoming bad company has an impact not only on the one who hosts them but also on those who follow their example.

It is so important to seek the Lord's wisdom regarding the company you keep and the worldly temptations that draw your attention away from your anointing and purpose. Keep your focus on Him—listen and obey!

Has there been a time when you discovered that you were spiritually blind?

Have you come to realize that you are not to participate in some of the relationships in your life?

What did you do to resolve the issue? Or have you done anything?

_____

_____

_____

Have there been other associations (money, fame, etc.) that have caused you to become spiritually blind?

_____

_____

_____

NINETEEN

Whose Portrait Is This?

> But Jesus, knowing their evil intent, said, "You hypocrites, why are you trying to trap me? Show me the coin used for paying the tax." They brought him a denarius, and he asked them, "Whose image is this? And whose inscription?" "Caesar's," they replied. Then he said to them, "So give back to Caesar what is Caesar's, and to God what is God's." When they heard this, they were amazed. So they left him and went away.
>
> *Matthew 22:18–22*

The Jewish expectation of the Messiah was that He would be a political leader who would deliver them from Roman occupation. When Jesus talked about God's Kingdom, they listened through their own worldview and agenda and assumed this Kingdom was a political one where Israel would be free of the Romans once again.

Early in their journey together, Jesus' disciples began to ask Him about His Kingdom. After the resurrection, they were still asking the same questions! "They gathered around him and asked him, 'Lord, are you at this time going to restore the kingdom to Israel?'" (Acts 1:6). This was after He had taught them again about

His Kingdom for forty days, in addition to what He had told them for more than three years. "He appeared to them over a period of forty days and spoke about the kingdom" (Acts 1:3).

The Lord used this opportunity to help them understand the spiritual Kingdom and their responsibilities in advancing the Kingdom of God by saying,

> It is not for you to know the times or dates the Father has set by his own authority. But you will receive power when the Holy Spirit comes on you; and you will be my witnesses in Jerusalem, and in all Judea and Samaria, and to the ends of the earth.
>
> Acts 1:7–8

Please note, He didn't say He would establish His Kingdom somewhere else; rather, He told them it simply was not the time for them to know when it would be established. Their calling was to demonstrate the power of the spiritual Kingdom by the power of the Holy Spirt.

This belief that the Messiah would free Israel from Rome was deeply engraved in their spirits. If, in fact, this was the mindset of the disciples, it's not hard to imagine the thinking of the secular Jews of that time was much the same. They even tried to make Him their political king by force. "Jesus, knowing that they intended to come and make him king by force, withdrew again to a mountain by himself" (John 6:15).

Since the people were not successful in making Him their king or convincing Him to deliver them from their political rulers, they tried to trap Him by accusing Him of something for which He could be arrested. "Then the Pharisees met together to plot how to trap Jesus into saying something for which he could be arrested" (Matthew 22:15 NLT). They selected men from among their followers and sent them to where Jesus was teaching to ask Him different questions about tax issues, marriage, the resurrection, the greatest commandment, etc.

Their first question was a political question to disqualify Him as a spiritual leader and to create conflict between Him and the Roman civil government. To accomplish this, their first strategy was to ask Him a question that would force Him to choose between the law of God and the Roman government. The question was related to taxes. "Tell us then what You think about this: Is it lawful to pay tribute [levied on individuals and to be paid yearly] to Caesar or not?" (Matthew 22:17 AMPC).

The Pharisees wanted to create a problem for the Lord Jesus by asking this legal question, and He knew that. "But Jesus, knowing their evil intent, said, 'You hypocrites, why are you trying to trap me?'" (Matthew 22:18). The amazing thing was they didn't respond to His question. They usually complained by saying that He was insulting them. This time, their evil intention was hidden behind a cunning ploy that was publicly uncovered. That must have been an uncomfortable moment.

One of the most important principles the Pharisees overlooked was that God could see and evaluate human motives. He searches motives and examines hearts. Before Jesus heard what their question was, He had already seen their motives and intentions. God sees everything; nothing is hidden from His eyes. Such awareness protects the children of God from saying or doing the wrong things and encourages walking with integrity of heart. Integrity of heart means you are living a life that honors God, both in public and in private, without hypocrisy. Hidden motives are the enemy of our spiritual reality, since our calling is to be the light of the world.

The strongest words the Lord Jesus used during His earthly ministry were said when He warned against the hypocritical life the Pharisees displayed (see Matthew 23). In the Kingdom of God, it is not *what* we say but *why* we say it that matters. It is not what we do, but why we do it. After Jesus exposed their concealed motives, He asked them to show Him the coin used for paying taxes to Caesar. They didn't understand what He was doing, but with curiosity, they gave Him a denarius.

Jesus asked, "Whose image and inscription is this?" They replied that it was Caesar's image. It was this probing dialogue that the Pharisees tried to avoid through their disguised questions and hidden motives. On hearing their response, Jesus established the difference between the kingdom of Caesar and His Kingdom, which is the Kingdom of light, life, righteousness, peace, joy, power in the Holy Spirit, justice, and an eternal destination. He told them how to live if they wanted the full manifestation of the Kingdom of light by saying, "Pay therefore to Caesar the things that are due to Caesar, and pay to God the things that are due to God'" (Matthew 22:21 AMPC).

The first part of His question, "Whose portrait is this?" was about ownership. The portrait was the image of the owner. It was permanent branding. There was no question about who owned it or whose property it was. They told the Lord the portrait and the inscription on the coin were Caesar's. The case was settled, since God was not interested in what belonged to Caesar. Furthermore, the earth and all its fullness belong to the Lord (see Psalm 24:1–2). These wicked religious elitists were trapped by their own question!

The Lord Jesus came to be the Light of the world to reveal the hidden work of darkness in people's lives, in religious systems (like the Pharisees'), and in politics. Their intention was to limit His light from shining by creating confusion. It is so important to notice that the Lord didn't tell the people to avoid paying taxes to the Roman government. Instead, He showed them how to operate in a political kingdom with the authority and power of the Kingdom of God.

The most important question is, Whose mark are you carrying? As His child, you are called to carry His image, to reflect His glory daily, and to bring what belongs to Him—your life, which is bought by the blood of the Lord Jesus—as a living sacrifice. The seal you carry shows who should own your life, your skills, your time, and your resources. As children of God who are sealed by the Holy Spirit, we belong to Him, and everything we have is His. The Lord's word is straightforward: "Give to God what is God's!"

The best place to start is by separating what is Caesar's (human) from what belongs to God. When we sort it out, we can give it to the rightful owner. This includes everything in our lives. That is how we live for His glory and enjoy His presence daily. Just remember that a thief can't enjoy the presence of a person he or she is stealing from. Not giving God what belongs to Him quenches the fire of the Holy Spirit in your life, and it becomes a hindrance to His manifested presence.

Whose mark are you carrying?

Do you believe you carry His seal in your spirit?

Are you willing to give Him what is rightfully His and live for His glory?

Are you truly walking as the light in following Jesus?

TWENTY

Can These Bones Live?

> The hand of the LORD was upon me, and he brought me out by the Spirit of the LORD and set me in the middle of a valley; it was full of bones. He led me back and forth among them, and I saw a great many bones on the floor of the valley, bones that were very dry. He asked me, "Son of man, can these bones live?" I said, "Sovereign LORD, you alone know."
>
> *Ezekiel 37:1–3*

Hope is one of the greatest gifts God gives to His people. True vision creates hope and restores hope. Since hope is focused on the future, it can't be separated from a true and clear vision about the future.

The question the Lord asked the prophet Ezekiel was challenging because of the reality and the condition of Israel at that time. Things really couldn't have been worse. The Lord took Ezekiel to show him that reality. Ezekiel was taken to the valley of dry bones by the hand of the Lord, which means there was divine guidance and initiative in this visit. The tour guide was the Holy Spirit.

Recently, my wife and I went with some friends to visit Unity Park in Ethiopia. We spent about five hours there and enjoyed the visit very much—mainly because of our tour guide. Our tour guide was a young man who was very knowledgeable and passionate about the history of his nation. What impressed me the most was that he was filled with hope about the future of the country, even while he was showing us the destruction that socialism had brought to the nation. He took us beyond the historical destruction of the past and helped us to see the future through his eyes. For me, sharing in his hope for his nation was the highlight of our trip and an awesome experience.

That's what the Holy Spirit did for Ezekiel. He took him to the valley to show him the history and the results of Israel's sin. But He did not leave him in that hopeless valley. He wanted to give hope for an expected future. He wanted to show Ezekiel His vision. God showed him that he would move from the valley of dry bones to a mighty army of God that was forming. That shift moved Ezekiel from the valley of defeat to the mountain of victory; from the state of confusion to a place of unity; from disorder to divine order; from the valley of fear to the mountain of faith; and from hopelessness to the place where he could see the future promises of divine blessings (see Ezekiel 36–37).

For Ezekiel to come out of the valley of despair, however, the Holy Spirit wanted him to answer God's question, obey His voice, and accept His mandate. This is the designated path of victory for every believer, family, church, and nation.

The valley of dry bones represented the condition of Israel without God. God showed him the result of rebelling against God and breaking His covenant, destroying His altar, and rejecting His voice. Elijah described the situation as, "The Israelites have rejected your covenant, torn down your altars, and put your prophets to death with the sword. I am the only one left, and now they are trying to kill me too" (1 Kings 19:10). These dry and scattered bones were a metaphor for the soul of the nation, and it appeared that there was no possibility of coming back to life. They were dry, lifeless, without future hope, scattered, without any identity or unity. No one could tell what was what or who was who.

Ezekiel went back and forth among the bones and the reality sank in. Israel's future looked bleak. At the end of the tour the Lord asked, "Son of man, can these bones live?" In other words, is there any hope that these lifeless, very dry, and scattered pieces of bones without any identification will live again? Will they live again to become a person, a family, a community, or a nation?

Humanly speaking, he couldn't say, "Yes, they can live again," or "There is hope." Their condition was very clear. How should he answer? His answer was, "Sovereign LORD, you alone know." I like his answer. Only God knows! Only He has the answer and the solution to this very difficult and impossible challenge. This is true not only because of His creative and redeeming power but also because of His great mercy and unchanging covenant. He is the only one who can say, "For I am the LORD, I do not change; therefore you are not consumed, O sons of Jacob" (Malachi 3:6 NKJV).

"You alone know" is our password when we need access to a true and lasting solution to unsolvable problems and to difficult questions in life. He is the only one who can say, "I am the LORD, the God of all mankind. Is anything too hard for me?" (Jeremiah 32:27). The answer is that nothing is too hard for Him.

Here's the catch: the primary purpose of God's question was not that He was looking for a specific, correct answer. He wanted to demonstrate the result of sin and human limitation and to show His power. "That power is the same as the mighty strength he exerted when he raised Christ from the dead" (Ephesians 1:19–20).

The command of the Lord was simple: Prophesy to the dry bones to live again. "Then he said to me, 'Prophesy to these bones and say to them, "Dry bones, hear the word of the LORD"'" (Ezekiel 37:4). The Lord wanted His prophet to be a part of the resurrection and restoration process. Ezekiel was asked to prophesy to the dry and scattered bones that filled the valley.

It was one thing to have the faith required to prophesy to individuals, a group of people, communities, and nations, but it was a totally different challenge to prophesy to bones and command them to live again. If he would prophesy the word of the Lord to his audience of dry bones, the Lord would start acting upon His word by giving them breath and life.

As Ezekiel obeyed the Lord, the power of the word of the Lord started to work, and it brought about restoration of hope by creating movement. Ezekiel saw the result of his obedience by faith. Now the Lord asked him to prophesy to what he couldn't see—the life-giving Spirit of God for resurrection and life. The greatest hope in human history was resurrected, which brought revival, renaissance, rebirth, restoration, renewal, and revitalization.

The lesson is the same for you and me today. It is not enough to believe in the ability of God. We must understand the holiness of God in order to repent for the full restoration of hope and the resurrection to receive life again. That is how we start our walk with the Lord. This takes place through repentance by recognizing the fruit of our sin, which is death.

When you answer His question and understand the result of your sin, God extends His grace of salvation, restoration, and resurrection by sending the life-giving wind of the Holy Spirit to dwell among and in you and as His temple.

When you submit to His will by declaring His word over the dry bones in your life, you will be restored. That is what makes you part of His army to fight spiritual warfare for the salvation, restoration, and deliverance of others, as you prophesy the eternal truth and declare the power of the Gospel of the Kingdom with determination and urgency. Your bones can live again if you obey by faith. The army of the Kingdom will rise up, and the Body of Christ will be reunited as His bride for that final day.

Have you spoken to the dry bones or places in your life?

Do you believe that God can bring those areas back to life?

Are you willing to repent to see hope revitalized in your life?

Is there anything else you need to do to see your bones live?

TWENTY-ONE

What Is in Your Hand?

> Then the LORD said to [Moses],
> "What is that in your hand?"
> *Exodus 4:2*

Moses is an example of how you can discover more about your assignment when you uncover the authority God has placed on your life. The human tendency for people under assignment is to begin searching for provision outside, but the Lord starts with what He has already deposited in you. You do not need to go shopping for the resources that come with your assignment. God starts the implementation process with the question "What is in your hand?" Or, "What do you have?" It doesn't matter how much or how little you have in the beginning, because His plan includes resources. He prepares in advance what you will need to fulfill the assignment.

Now, a clear vision establishes a value system that helps organizations, ministries, and businesses be strong and purposeful. If you go to any organization's website, you will likely find their vision statement. Vision provides direction to make a dream a reality and encourages implementation of a plan. True vision is the ability to see the resources God has prepared in advance. Most of the time, it requires divine intervention for us to see what God has already arranged.

When the Lord gave Moses the vision of the burning bush, the first command from the Lord was for Moses to take off his shoes; he was in the presence of the holy God. After Moses took off his shoes, the Lord revealed His strategy for Moses and the people of Israel. This was going to be a partnership with God, and God held all the resources Moses needed to take the people to the Promised Land.

Moses started explaining his lack of resources and his weaknesses, trying to argue that he was not the right person to lead the people. He continued to seek external resources to lead Israel. Finally, the Lord stopped Moses and asked, "What is in your hand?" All Moses had in his hand was his staff.

You don't have to exaggerate what you have for the Lord to be able to use it. All the Lord wants is for you to look and tell Him the truth. You should be able to see what is *in your hands*, even if you can't see or believe what is in you. Using what is in your hands builds your confidence as you realize what God has placed *in you*.

When Moses told the Lord what was in his hand, the Lord gave him instructions on what to do with it. The best way to multiply the insignificant things in your life to accomplish great things for God is to follow His guidance. The Lord told Moses to drop his staff to the ground.

Moses had used that staff for self-protection in the wilderness. He also had used the same staff to lead the sheep of his father-in-law for forty years. That staff had supported him, protected him, and been a critical tool in his daily work. To drop that staff meant letting go of his support system, self-defense mechanism, and familiar way of doing things. It also was a practical lesson in trusting the Lord. This is not easy for anyone.

When Moses let go of his staff, however, it was transformed for a greater purpose. It changed into a serpent, and Moses ran from it because it was unfamiliar to him. Then the Lord told him to pick it up, which probably sounded like a horrible idea, but Moses knew how to handle the staff. Once you give what is in your hands to the Lord, it becomes a sign of authority in the Lord's hands. From the moment Moses' staff changed into a snake, it became God's sign of authority. The instant Moses obeyed and picked it up again, the snake once again became a staff.

When a leader gives to the Lord what is in his or her hands, the Lord blesses it and gives it back to them. The Lord gave Moses' staff back to him after He made it the rod of authority. Stewardship is the ability to manage and use for the glory of God what God has blessed and given back.

Giving what is in your hands to the Lord is a test of your faith, while faithfully giving to others what He puts in your hands is a test of our character. A life of impact is the direct result of an individual's willingness to give back to the Lord what he or she has and to pass that gift on to the next generation.

An impoverished widow came to Elisha and begged for the lives of her sons (see 2 Kings 4). A creditor was ready to take her sons to make them slaves, and she was desperate. After he heard her cry, Elisha asked her what she had in her home. She told him that she didn't have anything except for a little oil in a jar. That small amount was all the Lord needed to deliver the next generation. Elisha told her to go and borrow as many empty jars as she could from her neighbors.

After the widow reported that her home was full of empty jars, the prophet of God told her to close the door behind her and her sons. Then she and her sons were to pour the little oil she had into the empty jars until every jar was filled. The oil didn't run out or stop until she filled all the jars. The flow only gave out when her sons told her there was not another empty jar left. When she reported to Elisha the miracle that had taken place, he told her to sell the oil, pay the creditor, and live on what remained.

The size of what we have is not important to the Lord; the amount of oil the widow had was small, but the oil was pure. It was not diluted with water. For God to multiply what we have, it has to be pure. For God, the issue is not how big the provision is, but how pure it is.

God uses what is in a leader's hand—trumpets, jars, torches, or a staff. Samson delivered his people with a donkey's jawbone (see Judges 15:16). Gideon had only his inner strength, and to be honest, he was in hiding when the Lord called him (see Judges 6:12–16). His clan was renowned for being the weakest in Manasseh, and he was the least in his family, but God shaped him into a mighty warrior because of the calling on his life and the inner strength he had.

When you are full of godly vision and are willing to give by faith to the Lord what is in your hand, you can accomplish great things for God. What is in your heart helps you to obey, while what is in your hands enables you to act. When God works with you, even the smallest thing you give back to the Lord in true obedience accomplishes much.

The Lord Jesus Christ, the greatest leader to ever live, started His mission as a humble carpenter who gave up everything. Yet He had received a portion that was enough to save humanity. Jesus received the name that is above every name and is above all authority on earth, in the heavens, and beneath the earth. To serve God's purpose among this generation requires stewarding God's resources in your heart and hand. It's not an option, but a part of your life and a mark of your leadership.

What is in your hand and heart?

_____

_____

_____

How willing are you to give to the Lord?

What have you received from the Lord that you are passing to the next generation to make a difference?

Do you understand the power and the authority that God has placed within you?

Has the Holy Spirit revealed to you what is in your hand to fulfill God's plans and purposes for your life?

TWENTY-TWO

Who Is This Who Questions My Wisdom?

> Who are you to question my wisdom with
> your ignorant, empty words?
>
> *Job 38:2* GNT

In a court of law, eyewitnesses are asked to testify as to what they heard, saw, smelled, or touched. These witnesses are expected to tell the truth before the judge and jury to establish what really happened.

Throughout Scripture, the Lord also instructed His people to settle matters with two or three witnesses (see Deuteronomy 19:15). Jesus reiterated the same principle when He said, "But if they will not listen, take one or two others along, so that 'every matter may be established by the testimony of two or three witnesses'" (Matthew 18:16). This was also the reason Paul instructed the young leader Timothy by saying, "Do not entertain an accusation against an elder unless it is brought by two or three witnesses" (1 Timothy 5:19).

Two or three people witnessing the same thing is one of the most powerful and indisputable ways to establish truth and corroborate a story. That is why it was upheld throughout the Old Testament, in the gospels, and in the letters to the Church as a solid proof of truth for any trial. The twelve apostles of Jesus were chosen to be the eyewitnesses of the resurrection of the Lord Jesus Christ. The apostle John summarized this by saying, "The life appeared; we have seen it and testify to it, and we proclaim to you the eternal life, which was with the Father and has appeared to us" (1 John 1:2).

In the Bible, we read about a few individuals and scenarios where the Lord, as the witness, testified about their character. King David was called a man after God's own heart. He faithfully served God's purpose in his own generation and received God's promise for a lasting dynasty (see Acts 13:21–22).

Noah acted by faith in the fear of the Lord to save his family in the midst of a very demonic and evil generation. It was such a horrible and lawless time that the Lord chose to start from scratch. God was going to send a flood to wipe out the entire world except for one man and his family. "But Noah found favor in the eyes of the LORD. This is the account of Noah and his family. Noah was a righteous man, blameless among the people of his time, and he walked faithfully with God" (Genesis 6:8–9). That passage demonstrates God vouching for, or witnessing to, the character of His servant. Noah went on to become a preacher of righteousness in his fallen generation for 120 years while he was building an ark until God's judgement fell on the world in the form of the great flood.

Of all the Bible characters, the person who received the highest praise from the Lord was Job. We watch a dramatic scene in heaven where Satan visits the Lord, and the two of them have a discussion. The Lord said to Satan, the accuser, "Have you considered my servant Job? *There is no one on earth like him*; he is blameless and upright, a man who fears God and shuns evil" (Job

1:8, emphasis added). What a testimony! The Lord didn't just say that Job was blameless, was upright, and feared God, but He said that there was no one on earth like him. What an amazing and awesome character witness God became for Job. God knows and sees everything from the beginning to the end. He examines not only our actions but also our inner motives.

One of the most beautiful characteristics that God highlighted in Job's life was that Job was a worshiper. He was a man of prayer, not only for himself, but also for his family. The second significant characteristic was that he worshiped the Lord in the middle of indescribable suffering and pain. "At this, Job got up and tore his robe and shaved his head. *Then he fell to the ground in worship*" (Job 1:20, emphasis added).

When we start with worship, we are prepared to overcome problems and challenges. Noah worshiped and walked in the fear of the Lord for 120 years. After surviving the flood, he continued worshiping by building an altar for the Lord. "Then Noah built an altar to the LORD and, taking some of all the clean animals and clean birds, he sacrificed burnt offerings on it" (Genesis 8:20).

Daniel continued worshiping the Lord in the middle of persecution, knowing he would be thrown into the lions' den. After he was thrown into the lions' den, the king came early in the morning and said, "Daniel, servant of the living God, has your God, whom you serve continually, been able to rescue you from the lions?" (Daniel 6:20). The answer was yes. "My God sent his angel, and he shut the mouths of the lions" (verse 22).

While it was true that Job walked in integrity and worshiped the Lord through all of the pain, he was tempted to stop his worship when he lost all of his children in one day, suddenly and without any warning or explanation. When he was afflicted with painful sores all over his body, he still feared and honored God. When his wife told him to stop worshiping God, to curse Him, and to die because of his suffering, Job didn't stop trusting and honoring

God. He praised the Lord by saying, "The LORD gave and the LORD has taken away; may the name of the LORD be praised" (Job 1:21). In spite of all this, "Job did not sin by charging God with wrongdoing" (Job 1:22). He worshiped Him.

The most difficult thing for Job, however, even more than the destruction of his properties, the death of his children, the discouraging words of his wife, the condemnation and a lecture from his friends, was not understanding what was happening and why it was happening. As humans, we like to know why things are happening. We like to ask why, how, when. It is very difficult to be still and know God is in the middle of a raging storm.

When Job began to lament his situation and ask questions, the Lord responded with a question of His own. "Who is this that questions my wisdom with such ignorant words?" (Job 38:2 NLT). Instead of explaining everything to us, God encourages us to trust His knowledge and walk by faith. We can only please Him when we walk by faith. Job waited on the Lord, and he had unwavering faith and hope.

He did not know that God had given Satan permission to test him. He did not know this test was for his promotion. He did not know God's plan for him. He was completely in the dark about what was going on, which caused him to ask questions. He felt that he was walking in integrity of character and attitude, and he assumed he was being punished unjustly. He didn't realize how limited his knowledge was until the end. Like many you see in the Bible, being able to worship and staying strong in your faith is what pleases God. These two things alone will bring about the needed change to have things restored as Job did.

God reveals to you not necessarily what you would like to know, but what you need to know to live for His glory. As Moses put it, "The secret things belong to the LORD our God, but the things revealed belong to us and to our children forever, that we may follow all the words of this law" (Deuteronomy 29:29).

Have you been in a situation where you didn't understand why you were experiencing trials?

Have you ever questioned God with the why, how, when, where, etc.?

During your hardship, did you continue to worship the Lord?

Were you able to keep your eyes on the Lord and walk in faith?

Looking back, what would you change or do differently?

PART FOUR

QUESTIONS OF VISION

Vision is our ability to see what is not here yet. Vision provides a strong foundation for value and strategic planning, and it gives a person direction, hope, and anticipation. The source of godly vision is God Himself. Aim to see God, see what He sees, and see things the way He sees them.

TWENTY-THREE

What Do You See?

> The word of the LORD came to me: "What do you see, Jeremiah?" "I see the branch of an almond tree," I replied.
> *Jeremiah 1:11*

Clear vision is a necessary foundation for your walk. You need godly vision to see both your potential and the possibilities from God's perspective for a greater impact to fulfill your calling.

God's question about ministry usually starts with vision. He asks, *What do you see?* Our human tendency is to jump into what we think needs to be done. *Doing* is more appealing to our nature than *seeing* what's happening in our ourselves and our surroundings. The truth is that who you are is more important to God than what you can do. How you see yourself, as well as what you see, matters to God.

Your territories or boundaries are marked by your vision. In other words, you won't go too far beyond your personal vision. A lack of vision limits your effectiveness far more than a lack of resources or skills because the ability to see clearly begins with your view of God and of yourself. You cannot go beyond the limits of your own beliefs and vision, which is why it is so important to see yourself as God sees you.

When the call of God came to a young, emerging leader named Jeremiah, he looked internally and evaluated himself first. His response to God's calling to be a prophet to the nations was "I am a child" (Jeremiah 1:6 ASV). Jeremiah was looking at his own abilities and skills, trying to see if he could step into this leadership role as a prophet of the nations. But don't all leaders say something along the lines of, "I'm just ___" as they take stock of their personal inventory?

Only God knows your true potential, and only He can direct you down the path He has preplanned for you. God's message to Jeremiah was *Look at My prepared plan for your life before you look at your abilities, skills, experiences, and everything else.* The Lord, who set apart and appointed Jeremiah before he was born, had already provided what Jeremiah needed to fulfill his destiny. Hence, his leadership responsibility was looking into *and accepting* what God had already done to equip him before he led others.

He has given you a purpose and a calling. The term *calling* in this context is when God moves you from where you have been to where you should be so that He can send you to do His will. This is why it all begins by being, not by doing. The source of true confidence comes from knowing yourself and believing what God has done. Accepting your personal identity gives you greater authority.

Consider the apostle Paul's reflection about his leadership abilities. "But by the grace of God I am what I am, and his grace to me was not without effect. No, I worked harder than all of them—yet not I, but the grace of God that was with me" (1 Corinthians 15:10). Effectiveness in your calling begins with knowing who God is, knowing who you are in God, and accepting His preplanned provision through faith and obedience.

God reminded Jeremiah that what he needed to be an effective leader was a divine touch. The touch of God brings about personal transformation, and a transformed life is required if your mission is to transform others (see Jeremiah 1:9–10). In biblical history, every leader who was touched by the Lord was transformed. Jacob was transformed when he saw the Lord face-to-face and was touched by Him (see Genesis 32:23–32). Isaiah was set free from guilt and continued his prophetic ministry as one of the greatest Old Testament prophets when the angel touched his mouth with a purifying fire (see Isaiah 6:1–7). The apostles John, James, and Peter were touched and transfigured by the Lord at the Mount of Transfiguration (see Matthew 17:1–13). We know that the touch of God transforms lives, purifies mouths, and opens eyes for clearer vision. When the Lord touched Jeremiah's mouth, he received everything he needed to be a prophet to the nations.

God also reminded Jeremiah about walking in obedience rather than scrambling to possess what he believed he needed to be successful in his calling. The key is to walk in obedience and trust in God for every provision. The Lord said, "Do not say, 'I am too young.' You must go to everyone I send you to and say whatever I command you" (Jeremiah 1:7).

God also reminded Jeremiah of his greater need for vision over provision. What you see is more important than what you think because being effective is more about vision than a set of skills. The question that asks what you see is fundamental, especially if you are called to be a leader who will correct history as Jeremiah did. The challenge becomes "See, today I appoint you over nations and kingdoms to *uproot and tear down, to destroy and overthrow*, to build and to plant" (Jeremiah 1:10, emphasis added). The actions of uprooting and tearing down, destroying and overthrowing involve dealing with what is wrong. Building and planting are about the future. In order for a leader to be able to carry out such responsibilities, he or she needs to have clear vision, strong values, and a tested character.

As God's servant, you can't just have a personal understanding of your life and ministry's vision. You must also understand how your personal revelation of Christ will have an impact on your ministry's present and future development. In the end, "What do you see?" can only be answered in the context of "*Who* do you see?"

Even though Jeremiah had believed he was too young, through his faith and trusting God, he did what he was shown and walked in complete victory. The same can be true for you if you follow his example.

What do you see? Or who do you see as the head of your life or ministry?

Do you know what God's preplanned purpose or calling is for you?

Do you see the vision clearly?

Do you walk in obedience to the Lord?

Do you have a real trust in your relationship with God?

TWENTY-FOUR

Whom Shall I Send?

> Then I heard the voice of the Lord saying, "Whom shall I send? And who will go for us?" And I said, "Here am I. Send me!"
> *Isaiah 6:8*

God's questions are not about fact finding or information gathering for a sound decision-making purpose. He doesn't need to investigate anything; He knows it all. Instead, His questions are meant to create awareness, to bring forth a greater and deeper revelation, and to provide knowledge and wisdom that can lead a person to transform and fulfill His will on earth.

Another reason God asks the questions He does is to find people who will commit to glorifying Him by doing His will. In this regard, the most powerful and direct question is the one God asked the prophet Isaiah: *Whom shall I send, and who will go for Me?* The core of the question is who. In other words, who is available and willing to obey His will?

The first part of the question relates directly to your availability. The Lord is always seeking a person after His own heart that He can send to do His will. The second part relates to your willingness to obey. God is looking for an individual who is willing to pay the price to do His will by accepting the call of God on his or her life. The two-part question, therefore, shows that God is looking for people who will go willingly and joyfully in obedience to the voice of God and are committed to the will of the Father, even if it is costly.

At the time that Isaiah was writing the verses above, Israel's spiritual condition was very disappointing, to say the least. The list of their sins against God included breaking the covenant, rebelling against God, not knowing Him, not realizing His provision, continuing in sin, forgetting God in their daily lives, turning their backs on Him, becoming transgressors and doers of evil, giving in to corruption, and becoming like Sodom and Gomorrah (see chapters 1–5).

The Lord summarized the spiritual condition of the nation in the parable of the vineyard. The vineyard was barren and fruitless despite the care that was given to it. "The nation of Israel is the vineyard of the LORD of Heaven's Armies. The people of Judah are his pleasant garden. He expected a crop of justice, but instead he found oppression. He expected to find righteousness, but instead he heard cries of violence" (Isaiah 5:7 NLT).

God granted Isaiah a vision (see Isaiah 6). In the year that King Uzziah died, and in the middle of preaching against sin and the spiritual disorder of the nation of Israel, Isaiah received a vision. In this vision, Isaiah saw the Lord seated on a lofty throne while the train of His robe filled the temple (see Isaiah 6:1). The Lord showed His prophet His greatness. In spite of the declining spiritual condition of the nation and the death of the king who had ruled the nation for 52 years, the true King was on the throne, and He was clothed in majesty.

The role of a king during that time was very important. Kings were considered the shepherds who had a mandate to protect, to lead, and to defend their people. When he became king at the age of sixteen, Uzziah began with the fear of the Lord and followed the spiritual guidance that was given to him. He followed the footsteps of his father, and even went beyond that by seeking the Lord and receiving instruction from the prophet Zechariah. Zechariah's instructions were foundational but simple—fear the Lord and seek Him. He obeyed and sought the fear of the Lord.

Uzziah, however, failed to remain accountable. When he stopped seeking the Lord, three things took over his life. The first one was pride. The second was self-sufficiency. And when he became famous because of the Lord's protection and provision, he lost the fear of the Lord. The third one was unfaithfulness. He began to act as if he was indispensable, which led him into entitlement.

When he was humble, Uzziah listened to one person and walked in the fear of the Lord and sought the Lord. When he became unfaithful to the Lord, he refused to listen to the voice of 81 priests. In anger, he entered the temple to burn incense to the Lord. At the altar, leprosy broke out on his forehead. Seeing this, they rushed him out of the temple.

Because of the pride of his heart, King Uzziah wanted to be both the king and high priest. The year he died, the Lord showed Isaiah the only true King on His throne, and His temple was filled with His glory. This powerful vision helped Isaiah focus on the greatness and holiness of the God of Israel. When he looked up, he saw the Lord on His throne in full authority, and in the temple, he saw His holiness and glory.

Undoubtedly, King Uzziah made the nation very vulnerable by creating a vacuum both politically and economically. He ruled the nation for a long time, and Israel depended upon him for security. Israel probably relied on him for spiritual renewal since he initially began his reign with the fear of the Lord.

When the Lord said, *Whom shall I send? And who will go for us?* He was asking for a person who understood His authority and His holiness. Understanding the authority of God provides a strong foundation for our faith and helps us walk in humility and boldness, which are the characteristics of a true messenger of the Lord.

Isaiah responded, "Here am I. Send me!" He saw and understood the following principles, which made him one of the most powerful prophets of the Old Testament. First, he understood the spiritual condition of the nation. Knowing the reality of a situation makes a messenger very effective and dependent upon God. Second, he witnessed the result of pride in the actions and life of King Uzziah. Third, he saw the Lord highly exalted in the middle of spiritual deterioration and the death of the king, the leader of the nation. Fourth, he realized that despite the actions of the people of God, there are holy angels who declare His holiness day and night. As important as we are to the Lord, we are not indispensable. If we don't obey Him, He still has multitudes to worship Him and do His will. Fifth, he knew that he needed the touch of the fire of God before he was sent. Sixth, he understood the importance of accepting the calling, not because of past experiences or the hope of success in the future, but for the sake of obeying the call of God. It is not the result but the process of obeying the will of God wholeheartedly. This is living for the revealed will of God.

In every generation God asks, *Who shall I send? Who will go for us?* When we understand His holiness, we will humble ourselves before Him and cry for cleansing. Then and only then can we hear His voice and reply, "Here I am to do Your will the rest of my life." When we do that, the Lord will send us with power and purpose to complete what He has entrusted to us.

What would your answer be if the Lord asked you, "Who shall I send?"

Have you ever had to come to the place where you could see you were operating out of a prideful heart?

If so, what did you do to correct it?

Do you have a revelation of the holiness of God?

TWENTY-FIVE

Am I Not the One Who Is Sending You?

> The LORD turned to him and said, "Go in the strength you have and save Israel out of Midian's hand. Am I not sending you?" "Pardon me, my lord," Gideon replied, "but how can I save Israel? My clan is the weakest in Manasseh, and I am the least in my family." The LORD answered, "I will be with you, and you will strike down all the Midianites."
>
> *Judges 6:14–16*

One of the most effective instruments the enemy uses against us is discouragement. When we are dejected, hopelessness takes over. Hopelessness opens a big door to fear. Fear takes away faith, hope, and love and replaces them with doubt. Losing faith shakes our foundation and distorts our core values. This makes us unstable since our prayers become ineffective, and part of what makes our prayers effective is the ability to believe and not doubt.

But when you ask, you must believe and not doubt, because the one who doubts is like a wave of the sea, blown and tossed by the wind. That person should not expect to receive anything from the Lord. Such a person is double-minded and unstable in all they do.

James 1:6–8

This cycle intensifies unbelief, which leads to doubt and takes away the joy of the Lord. Since the joy of the Lord is our strength in praising and worshiping God, doubt steals our true worship. That reinforces hopelessness since hope deferred makes the heart sick (see Proverbs 13:12). What a mess!

If you have a working concept of how the human body works, you know that your heart is the most important organ in your body because it facilitates the blood circulation your body needs day and night. This is what hope does for your daily life. Your heart gets sick when you stop anticipating or expecting, and you lose confidence about your future. Just as a person with a sick heart will die if they don't get the right treatment, so will a person who loses hope. We gain energy to live today because of the hope of tomorrow.

When you lose hope, you stop caring and loving. God commands you to love your God with all your heart. That is why the Word of God says, "And now these three remain: faith, hope and love. But the greatest of these is love" (1 Corinthians 13:13). Faith is the foundation for your Christian walk. Hope is the source of your energy to anticipate the future or envision your future. When you have faith and hope, you start living a life of faith.

The formula of a God-honoring life and ministry is faith + hope = love. The Lord Jesus said, "As the Father has loved me, so have I loved you. Now remain in my love" (John 15:9). When you step out of the love of God, you lose faith and hope. Confusion and disappointment take over. Where there is no faith and hope, divine order cannot be expressed because faith works in love. The only thing that matters is faith expressing itself through love (see Galatians 5:6).

This was the condition of the Jewish people during the time of the judges, which started when the Israelites rejected the voice of the Lord and followed their own desires. "In those days Israel had no king; everyone did as they saw fit" (Judges 17:6). They abandoned the ways of God, so the Lord removed His protection. As a result, they were oppressed by their enemies. They felt they were abandoned by the Lord. They cried to the Lord in their suffering. So the Lord started raising up judges to deliver them.

Judges were military leaders who were sent by the Lord in response to the cry of the nation. He was sending His people a way to stop the destruction and their suffering. But the people didn't seek the Lord to worship Him and renew their relationship with Him as a holy, awesome God of the covenant. They cried to Him to get relief.

It is here that we find Gideon. During one of these times that the Israelites cried out because of the oppression of the Midianites, the Lord sent a prophet with this message: "I said to you, 'I am the LORD your God; do not worship the gods of the Amorites, in whose land you live.' But you have not listened to me" (Judges 6:10). The Lord sent His angel to Gideon. In every generation, God selects a person to partner with in spite of the conditions of his or her society (Enoch, Noah, and Elijah are great examples). Notice how the Lord approached Gideon to set him apart for His work. The angel said, "The LORD is with you, mighty warrior" (Judges 6:12).

It was important for Gideon to hear that the Lord was with him because the spirit of abandonment was ruling the nation at that time. Yes, the Lord might turn His face from those who turn their backs to Him, but His presence is always with those whose hearts are with Him. For Gideon to become the solution to the problem of his nation, he needed to know the presence of God was with him. Throughout the Bible, that is the only assurance the Lord gave every leader who felt inadequate to be able to do His will, and it was truly all they needed.

God was with him for effectiveness, security, rest, protection, provision, and guidance to complete the call on his life. Even when he was hiding from the enemy, and they would destroy everything and bring devastation to the nation, Gideon was still faithful to provide for his family. God honored his diligent spirit during one of the most difficult conditions. It seems that the Lord was saying to Gideon, "I was watching how much you cared for your family by protecting the small seed to feed your household." The test of a true leader is his commitment to his family, before he shows commitment to his followers. Family without a father, church without a shepherd, and a nation without a leader can't be effective.

But Gideon's calling was also about his true identity. The first part of the angel's declaration was to reveal God's closeness, while the second part was to unveil what God had already deposited in Gideon for his life's calling. The Lord was saying, *I am, therefore, you are.* In other words, you have all you need. The angel revealed who Gideon was in the eyes of the Lord by calling him with his true identity—mighty warrior.

What made him a mighty warrior was not his experience or his ability. It was the presence of God. Gideon complained about the absence of God from the nation, but the Lord told him that He was with him because of His plan for his life and His covenant to never forsake Israel. Yes, knowing what God is doing among His people is important.

The most important thing for you and me, however, is to know and experience the presence of God in order to fulfill His purpose. When the angel of the Lord called Gideon a mighty warrior, the Lord revealed Himself to Gideon to commission him for his calling to deliver the people who were crying to the Lord because of the oppression of their enemy.

The assurance the Lord gave Gideon was "I will be with you" (verse 16). Gideon accepted his calling and started to live and act according to his prophetic name. When you recognize who is calling you, you will do the same.

Have you ever found yourself in a situation where God was asking you to do something beyond what you could imagine?

Did fear and doubt try to come in?

Did you struggle with feelings of hopelessness?

Were you able to accomplish what He told you? How did you (*He*) do it?

Did you feel God was with you?

TWENTY-SIX

What Are You Doing in the Cave?

> There [Elijah] went into a cave and spent the night. And the word of the LORD came to him: "What are you doing here, Elijah?"
>
> *1 Kings 19:9*

The ultimate test of anyone's effectiveness is not how he starts but how he finishes. Starting well is crucial, but only for the sake of finishing well. If we are not willing to pay the price to go the distance, we will not finish well.

Elijah started very well. We don't know much about his upbringing, but we do know that he was concerned about the glory of God. After seeing the moral decline and spiritual bankruptcy of Israel under idolatrous King Ahab and wicked Queen Jezebel, Elijah prayed a dramatic prayer. He prayed sincerely for the Lord to stop the rain of blessing on the land of Israel so that the people would know the source of their blessing was not the idol Baal, but instead the Lord God Almighty.

As James later noted in his letter to the early Church, "Elijah was a human being, even as we are. He prayed earnestly that it would not rain, and it did not rain on the land for three and a half years" (James 5:17). Because of his sincere prayer for the glory of God, the Lord answered his prayer and made Elijah a prophet over Israel with great authority.

God also saw Elijah on his knees in prayer. Being on your knees refers to both your prayer life and your total humility and dependence upon God. When God finds you with a pure heart, right motives, real humility, and dependence through a devoted prayer life, He trusts you with a higher level of authority. This is the reason the Lord gave Elijah the key to the heavens and trusted him with full authority.

After Elijah received the key to close and open the heavens, he began his leadership journey. The first journey took him to the palace of the king of Israel. This unknown prophet went straight from his knees to the palace of King Ahab. There, Elijah declared with full authority that he closed the heavens and there would not be any rain until he opened them again. King Ahab didn't believe Elijah at first. He probably thought Elijah was just one of those crazy prophets who didn't know what they were talking about. So Elijah took the key to the heavens with him and left.

At this point, the anticipation of what God had prepared for him must have been very high. Since the Lord gave Elijah the key to open and close the heavens, why wouldn't God prepare a comfortable place where Elijah could relax until the drought was over? It wasn't to be.

After Elijah delivered the message to Ahab, the Lord spoke to Elijah, saying, "Go from here and turn east and hide yourself by the brook Cherith, east of the Jordan. You shall drink of the brook, and I have commanded the ravens to feed you there" (1 Kings 17:3–4 AMPC). There was no comfortable shelter; there was not even a tent. There was no place to cook. There was no one to fellowship with.

The Lord fed Elijah by sending ravens to deliver food to him. Remember, this man was a Jewish prophet who could not touch or eat unclean things, but in this case, Elijah was not even given a chance to choose the kind of bird or animal he would like to kill and eat. An unclean bird, a raven, brought meat from "wherever" to him. We don't know how many meals Elijah took from the mouth or talons of the ravens, but he humbled himself and did what the Lord said to do. That is how he kept his authority. Elijah passed the test!

In the meantime, King Ahab searched for Elijah in every nation. He finally realized that Elijah *did* have the key to open or close the heavens to rain. If a leader has true authority and he can solve the problems of a society, even those who don't like him will eventually start looking for him. God anoints leaders to solve the problems of their society, and the only way to keep the anointing is through ongoing intimacy with the Lord and living a life of humility.

When the time was right to open the heavens, Elijah went back and revealed himself to King Ahab; however, before he prayed for the rain to fall once again, he ordered that the broken altar of the Lord be restored. He prayed for the fire of God to fall, and it fell mightily and consumed the sacrifice. After the Lord answered his prayer, Elijah commanded that all Baal worshipers be slaughtered. "Then Elijah commanded them, 'Seize the prophets of Baal. Don't let anyone get away!' They seized them, and Elijah had them brought down to the Kishon Valley and slaughtered there" (1 Kings 18:40). Then Elijah prayed for rain, and the drought of three and a half years was broken. The blessing of God returned to the nation.

Such a demonstration of the power of God, combined with the fact that Elijah killed all the Baal prophets, made Queen Jezebel very angry. She threatened to kill Elijah. After all the victory he had experienced, he was scared and ran for his life. He even asked the Lord to take his life. But the angel of the Lord came and fed him twice to strengthen him for a forty-day journey. Finally, after many days of traveling, he reached Horeb, the mountain of God, and went into a cave to spend the night.

That is when the Lord came and asked him, "What are you doing here, Elijah?" Although Elijah had great authority and a very impactful ministry, he was alone at this critical point. He had not prepared a successor from the next generation of leaders. This was not the season for Elijah to hide in a cave and hope to go home to glory. It was, instead, a time to prepare future leaders. There was still anointing in Elijah for kings and prophets.

The final evaluation for a leader is not the great organization he or she leaves behind—it is the prepared and anointed new leadership he or she has trained who will serve the purpose of God in their own generation. This is what it means to be accountable to the next generation. Elijah not only anointed his successor, Elisha, but trained him and imparted to him a double portion of his anointing. He prepared him as his son.

Now is the time for everyone who cares about the Kingdom of God to come out from the cave of self-sympathy and prepare the next generation of leaders for a double portion anointing. The question of this hour is "What are you doing in the cave?" You can't afford to hide in a cave while the next generation is waiting to be equipped, empowered, and set apart to serve God's purpose and their generation. Your legacy will be found in preparing your successor while there is still time to do so. Obey God and be willing to go!

Are you out of the cave and ready to prepare the next generation's leadership?

Is your focus to nurture your successor into a successful leader for greater impact?

Do you still have the key of authority you received on your knees?

Some don't have the key of true authority because they don't take the time to stay on their knees. Others give back the key to the Giver because they don't remain humble. Others don't like to be fed by ravens. *What about you?*

TWENTY-SEVEN

How Long Will You Mourn for Saul?

> The LORD said to Samuel, "How long will you mourn for Saul, since I have rejected him as king over Israel? Fill your horn with oil and be on your way; I am sending you to Jesse of Bethlehem. I have chosen one of his sons to be king."
>
> 1 Samuel 16:1

The question in this passage was from God and was directed to Samuel. As a high priest, prophet, and judge, Samuel was one the greatest leaders in Israel. He grew up serving the Lord in the temple under the high priest, Eli, but in many ways, the Lord raised Samuel for Himself. "I will raise up for myself a faithful priest, who will do according to what is in my heart and mind. I will firmly establish his priestly house, and they will minister before my anointed one always" (1 Samuel 2:35).

While Samuel was leading the priesthood, the people of Israel told the Lord they wanted a king just like the other nations. This grieved both Samuel and the Lord because Israel was essentially rejecting God's leadership. God told Samuel to go ahead and anoint a king for them. Samuel anointed Saul as the first king to rule the nation because Saul was Israel's choice; however, Saul grieved the Lord through his disobedience on more than one occasion.

After repeatedly disobeying the Lord, Saul was told through Samuel that God was rejecting him, and his kingdom was going to be given to his neighbor. As a priest and prophet, Samuel went to Saul and declared this message to him, which was the last time Samuel would see Saul. The relationship was severed.

Still, Samuel had a hard time letting Saul go. He had a difficult time anointing the new king the Lord prepared. The Lord asked Samuel the question "How long will you mourn for Saul, since I have rejected him as king over Israel?" Maybe we could ask ourselves the same question.

How long have you grieved over a person or situation? As noted in Ecclesiastes 3, there is a season for everything. In fact, the apostle Paul also told the Church that if they didn't know the season, they were wasting the grace of God (see 2 Corinthians 6:1–2). God releases His special favor and grace according to the season. When the favor of God is released, true transformation becomes a reality, which means we start thinking and acting differently. Grace and favor enable us to fulfill God's purpose and to maximize every opportunity to redeem the time.

In each season, we must learn how to let go of the past. The Lord's question for Samuel was "How long?" He didn't ask Samuel *why* he lamented for Saul. Instead, He wanted him to know it was time to stop dwelling on the past and move into the new. There is a time when we should express our concern about the past or the present; however, when we are obsessed by what happened in the past, we miss God's will for today. If you truly care about what is happening in your generation, you must separate yourself from familiar things and let go of what God has rejected. Only then will you be able to work within God's value system.

Samuel was mourning for Saul and was not ready to anoint the new king, so the Lord commanded Samuel to fill his horn and be on his way. The horn was used for carrying the oil of anointing. The fact that the Lord told Samuel to fill his horn meant that it had been empty. Filling the horn with oil is a symbol of readiness. Once the horn is filled with oil, careful handling is required.

Then the Lord told Samuel to be on his way. It was time, and he needed to be proactive in finding the next leader for the coming generation. The time for mourning and staying stuck was gone. Samuel didn't know David when he left for Bethlehem. The Lord commanded him to go to the house of Jesse, so he went by faith in obedience to the word of the Lord.

Going to anoint the next generation of leaders is a very frightening thing. First, those who are holding titles or positions may not like it. Second, there is the possibility of anointing the wrong person. (David had seven brothers; it would have been easy to make a mistake.) Third, it may not be easy to find God's chosen successor. Anointing the right person may require waiting for a while, until David "comes home." But obedience by faith has no substitute.

The Lord had prepared David before Samuel was sent, so David was waiting for Samuel to set him apart for his destiny. The Lord is the one who calls and anoints us, but He gives the responsibility of setting us apart to those who are in leadership positions. Here are some of the key things to remember about David's anointing.

- David was anointed by the will of God. God was the one who sought David. He was looking for a leader after His heart to steward His eternal purpose in that season.
- David was anointed to break the old order and usher in the new order. The time of King Saul was marked by a spirit of jealousy, envy, competition, disobedience, selfishness, and human choice. God raised and anointed David to break that jealous spirit so that leaders would live for the glory of God with full devotion to Him alone.

- David was anointed by God to establish a new covenant with his God. During Saul's reign, the covenant was not honored. God is looking for a new generation of leaders who understand and are committed to keeping the covenant with Him.
- God chose David and anointed him to accomplish His purposes among the people of covenant.

David corrected what went wrong during the reign of Saul by bringing the Ark of the Covenant back, which represented God's presence. Today, God is looking for those who will correct history again by bringing back His presence and covenant to churches, ministries, businesses, and nations.

David established a standard of excellence as a king. He was led by the Spirit of God and followed the words of the Lord all the days of his life. God is looking for those who are willing to do the same. The Lord seeks those who worship Him in spirit and in truth in spite of their titles and positions.

The Lord is changing the season, even as you are looking for a successor. The work of the Kingdom must have a new paradigm. Repeating history is not an answer for today's social, economic, and spiritual problems. God is seeking to empower new leaders who have the heart of God, the mind of Christ, the vision of the Kingdom, and proven character to correct the past to shape the future. Tomorrow is choosing its leaders today. You have both a moral and an ethical responsibility to invest in those who have a heart like David.

Are you ready to fill your horn with oil, to anoint the next generation of leaders?

Do you worship Him in spirit and in truth?

Are you ready to leave your past behind and move forward into the plan and calling God has for your life?

Do you recognize the season you are in right now?

PART FIVE

QUESTIONS OF AUTHORITY

The major thing that makes Christians different from others, both as individuals and as leaders, is their spiritual authority. We've been given all authority to fulfill His will on earth as we walk in victory by His delegated power.

The effectiveness of a Christian leader is greatly enhanced when he or she understands his or her sphere of authority and then applies it with a holy fear or reverence of God. This is the key to advancing His divine purposes on earth.

TWENTY-EIGHT

Why Do You Cry to Me?

> Then the LORD said to Moses, "Why are you crying out to me? Tell the Israelites to move on."
>
> *Exodus 14:15*

You and I are called by God to fulfill His purpose on earth through His power and authority. The sign of that authority is His anointing. What is anointing? It is the sign of God's presence that enables us to carry out what He has placed on our lives. The anointing sets us apart for the calling. If we desire to be effective throughout this process, we must observe certain fundamentals.

First, we have to *accept the call*. God reveals His calling and purposes in a variety of ways. Some people are called before they are born. The prophet Jeremiah is a great example of this. God knew him before he was formed in his mother's womb (see Jeremiah 1:5). Jeremiah's calling (prophet to the nations) was with a specific office (assignment). For Jeremiah to walk in his calling with authority and the approval of God, he had to receive what he needed for the assignment, which was much greater than his natural ability or resources. The Lord gave him approval, resources, authority, and vision by touching his mouth and inserting His words. After that, Jeremiah was equipped for the calling, and he started to walk in it with divine authority and power.

Samuel was also set apart from childhood. Samuel's mother, Hannah, cried out to the Lord for a child. She swore that she would dedicate a son the Lord provided her back to the Lord for His purposes (see 1 Samuel 1:1–20). God heard Hannah's prayer, and Samuel was dedicated to the Lord. He grew up in the temple surrounded by the religious elite and learned how to serve in the house of God. The Lord revealed Himself to Samuel while he was still a very young boy, and the calling was established. Samuel grew up with God's anointing and power to bring spiritual transformation as a prophet, high priest, and political leader. "And the boy Samuel continued to grow in stature and in favor with the LORD and with people" (1 Samuel 2:26).

The call of Samuel summarizes the three offices in the Old Testament, namely priest, prophet, and king. In His call to leadership, the Lord made His expectation very clear, especially for the leaders (priests and prophets) who led His leaders (kings). He raised them for Himself. Their responsibility was to do what was on the heart and mind of God. "I will raise up for myself a faithful priest, who will do according to what is in my heart and mind" (1 Samuel 2:35). Furthermore, He promised to establish the ones He calls. "I will firmly establish his priestly house, and they will minister before my anointed one always" (1 Samuel 2:35).

Paul confirms God's promise in the New Testament by saying, "The one who calls you is faithful, and he will do it" (1 Thessalonians 5:24). Acceptance of the calling releases you into your prophetic destiny, and it gives you divine approval by the power of the Spirit of God.

Here are some examples of biblical characters who received God's Spirit and were launched into their destinies with power and authority that went way beyond their own:

- Saul: "When Saul heard their words, the Spirit of God came powerfully upon him, and he burned with anger" (1 Samuel 11:6).
- David: "And from that day on the Spirit of the LORD came powerfully upon David" (1 Samuel 16:13).
- Othniel: "The Spirit of the LORD came on him, so that he became Israel's judge and went to war" (Judges 3:10).
- Gideon: "Then the Spirit of the LORD came on Gideon" (Judges 6:34).
- Jephthah: "Then the Spirit of the LORD came on Jephthah" (Judges 11:29).
- Samson: "The Spirit of the LORD came powerfully upon him" (Judges 14:6, 19; 15:14).
- Jahaziel: "Then the Spirit of the LORD came on Jahaziel" (2 Chronicles 20:14).
- Jesus: "Jesus returned to Galilee in the power of the Spirit" (Luke 4:14). "God anointed Jesus of Nazareth with the Holy Spirit and power" (Acts 10:38).
- The apostles: "But you will receive power when the Holy Spirit comes on you" (Acts 1:8).
- Paul: "Brother Saul, the Lord—Jesus, who appeared to you on the road as you were coming here—has sent me so that you may see again and be filled with the Holy Spirit" (Acts 9:17).
- John: "On the Lord's Day I was in the Spirit" (Revelation 1:10).

The second fundamental for being effective in our calling is *knowing the time*. We are to learn not only to wait upon the Lord to know His will and to understand how to complete the assignment, but also to discern when to do it. Doing the will of God at the right time gives us God's approval and anointing, and it releases His divine authority, power, and resources.

The New Testament leaders were in the process of preparation for more than three years, training to receive power and to become effective leaders. Their willingness to follow the Lord, to be prepared and wait for His timing, enabled them to receive the power of the Holy Spirit to have an impact in their generation and beyond.

For fruitfulness and lasting impact, the answer of *when* gives us a very solid foundation. The Word of God tells us, "There is a time for everything, and a season for every activity under the heavens" (Ecclesiastes 3:1). In other words, everything should be done at the right time, which can be one of the most challenging things. For Christians, that means there is a time to hear the calling of God. There is a time to be prepared for the call of God, which could be short or long depending on God's timetable. God is the only one who controls the time, since He knows what a person needs and for how long they will need it.

The final fundamental is to *obey the call*. Moses passed the test for his anointing by both waiting for and accepting the calling. He waited upon the Lord longer than all the other leaders in the Bible. He sensed his calling when he was young through the natural compassion he had for his people, the Hebrew slaves, but he didn't have a direct encounter with God until he was eighty years old. I can imagine that there were times when he felt very confused by the direction of his life. He had given up everything as a young man to suffer with the people of God, losing his title, pleasures, opportunities, and fame because of the fire of destiny in his life. He was later exiled to the wilderness. This former prince of one of the greatest kingdoms in history was relegated to watching his father-in-law's nomadic herd of sheep. Some might call that a fall from grace, but for Moses, it was a call into greatness.

Years later, Moses brought the people of Israel out of bondage in Egypt and led them to the banks of the Red Sea. Unfortunately, their captors had a change of heart, and Pharaoh sent a massive army to retrieve the slaves or kill them where they stood. The

Israelites were trapped between a huge body of water and a raging army, so Moses cried out.

God heard Moses' cry and visited him. "Then the LORD said to Moses, 'Why are you crying out to me? Tell the Israelites to move on'" (Exodus 14:15). God's question to Moses was *why*, because Moses had been given full authority over the enemy's power. The power of God that worked many miracles in Egypt was still with them in the form of a pillar of fire by night and a cloud by day. More than that, the staff or rod of authority and power was still in Moses' hand. God's power can't be measured according to the force of the enemy—it can be measured according to His presence.

From that day on, Moses relied on God's power to perform signs and wonders, which included bringing the people across the Red Sea and out of Egypt into freedom, worship, and enjoyment of the Promised Land.

God's question for everyone who is called and entrusted with divine authority is, *Why do you cry to Me instead of using your authority to remove the enemy of the destiny of My people?* In order to walk in our calling, we must always be aware of the timing. In every situation, we should maintain our passion for God and a compassionate heart for His people. We need to remain humble and stay in His presence. We need to love God with all our heart, mind, soul, and strength. We need to continue our daily prayer time and be willing to change and grow in the things of God. Our answers will come in the right time in the mighty name of Jesus.

The most important question is, What would it take to be trusted with such authority in the Kingdom to destroy the strong opposition and lead God's people to their destination?

Have you ever cried out to God?

Did He answer you?

Has there been a time you got ahead of God? What happened?

Are you willing to change and grow in order to accept the call?

TWENTY-NINE

Why Have You Fallen on Your Face?

> The LORD said to Joshua, "Stand up!
> What are you doing down on your face?"
>
> *Joshua 7:10*

One of the greatest gifts God gives to a nation, to a church, or to His people is a God-fearing leader. For God's people, good leaders are answers to prayer, and providing a God-honoring leader shows the compassion of God for His people.

In the history of the Israelites, Moses was a gift and an answer to the cry of the people because Moses was a deliverer, and his people were languishing under a heavy yoke. Joshua led the people into the Promised Land, or their inheritance. Samuel was a restorer of the prophetic voice. David was a gift to shepherd God's people. The Word says of David,

> He chose David his servant and took him from the sheep pens; from tending the sheep he brought him to be the shepherd of his people

Jacob, of Israel his inheritance. And David shepherded them with integrity of heart; with skillful hands he led them.

Psalm 78:70–72

Leading the people of God into a place of promise has two aspects to it: breakout and breakthrough. Moses brought them out of Egypt very successfully. The call of Moses as a deliverer was to break out the Israelites from the yoke of slavery; however, the people weren't ready, so God had to wait forty years to raise up Joshua. When the time came,

> After the death of Moses the servant of the LORD, the LORD said to Joshua son of Nun, Moses' aide: "Moses my servant is dead. Now then, you and all these people, get ready to cross the Jordan River into the land I am about to give to them—to the Israelites."
>
> Joshua 1:1–2

Even though Moses was the deliverer for *breakout*, Joshua's calling was to lead them into their promise, which was the *breakthrough*.

Moses encountered a face-to-face confrontation with all the forces of Egypt in order to facilitate breakout. Breakout occurs when a leader joins the Lord in fighting the enemy of God's people. Joshua, however, prepared the people for breakthrough. Breakthrough focuses on internal strength that comes from walking in holiness with God. It comes when a leader prepares his or her people to follow God in a new way. While Moses started with miracles and signs to show the power of God, Joshua's starting point was consecrating the people for what God was going to do for them. The call of Joshua was to deal with the internal enemy of the power of God, while Moses' calling was to fight external forces with God's authority.

One of the characteristics of an effective breakout leader is being able to prepare successors for breakthrough leadership. This was the relationship between Moses and Joshua. Joshua was prepared by Moses to assume the leadership role. He started his leadership training by becoming Moses' aide, and he served Moses until Moses died. "Then Moses set out with Joshua his aide, and Moses went up on the mountain of God" (Exodus 24:13). As he was serving Moses, Joshua, the son of Nun, was set apart to represent Ephraim's tribe.

As his first test of his leadership ability, Joshua was sent to scout out the land the Lord was giving them. He went with the leaders of each tribe, and when these twelve spies came back to give the report about the land to the leaders, they said, "We went into the land to which you sent us, and it does flow with milk and honey! Here is its fruit" (Numbers 13:27). What an amazing proof of God's promise! The saddest thing, however, is that after they presented this evidence to Moses and the people, ten of the twelve spies said, "But the people who live there are powerful, and the cities are fortified and very large" (Numbers 13:28). They gave a bad report, and fear melted the hearts of the people.

Joshua and Caleb, who were among the twelve, had a different spirit and trusted the Lord wholeheartedly. They tried to persuade the others not to rebel against God but go forward in faith and courage. Instead of repenting, however, the people tried to stone Joshua and Caleb. That day, the Lord in His anger sentenced judgment against them by saying, "For forty years—one year for each of the forty days you explored the land—you will suffer for your sins and know what it is like to have me against you" (Numbers 14:34). That generation—with the exception of Joshua and Caleb—died in the wilderness. While this was a rough beginning for Joshua's leadership journey, the Lord was with him and prepared him for the role.

The central goal of Moses' leadership was the demonstration and display of God's power to destroy the power of the enemy. The focus of Joshua's leadership was honoring and protecting the holy covenant of God. Moses finished his leadership journey by asking to see more of the wonder and glory of God. Joshua summed up his leadership journey by declaring he would forever worship God. "As for me and my family, we'll worship GOD" (Joshua 24:15 MSG).

Joshua walked in the Promised Land and saw with his own eyes the promises of God for the nation. He was also in the presence of God on the mountain with Moses for forty days and nights. It is one thing to believe the promise because of the evidence, but it is another thing to be in the presence of the Promise Giver Himself. Finally, after forty years of training and preparation, the Lord told Moses to commission Joshua in the presence of the people. At the commission, Joshua received what made him an effective and victorious leader for the rest of his life: the spirit of wisdom. He received this gift by impartation through Moses, which also released favor upon his leadership. The people obeyed him, and the Lord exalted him by His presence.

After the death of Moses, the Lord told Joshua to lead the people of Israel into the Promised Land by crossing over the Jordan River. At this point, Joshua fully stepped into the leadership role. As a breakthrough leader, his starting point was different from Moses' starting point. Moses started his leadership by performing wonders in Pharaoh's presence in his palace. Since Moses' leadership was about breakout, he started with the demonstration of power and authority through miracles, signs, and wonders.

Moses' leadership had not required the participation of the people—his leadership required their willingness to obey his command. But Joshua's situation was different. He was to lead the people into the Promised Land, and he was to secure the presence of God for the fulfillment of His promises. That required the Israelites' participation. Joshua had to command them to consecrate themselves in order for them to see the manifestation of God's presence and to experience their breakthrough. Even though they had waited for forty years to cross over to the land that they had been promised, they had to recognize and follow His divine principles before they could take that step.

God is calling for us to face both external forces to protect our calling and internal sin to secure the victory. The presence of God is the only assurance we have that we can have lasting victory. So it is very important to know when to stand up and clean the house—instead of crying because of setbacks. The victory is yours if you remove the hindrances to His manifested presence. God's question for you and me is, "What are you doing down on your face?"

Have you ever had to wait for years to see God's promise?

During that time did you ever "fall on your face" or give up?

What kept you going or changed your situation for you to stay in faith?

Did you have to experience both breakout and breakthrough?

THIRTY

Why Are You Standing Here?

> Now when He had spoken these things, while they watched, He was taken up, and a cloud received Him out of their sight. And while they looked steadfastly toward heaven as He went up, behold, two men stood by them in white apparel, who also said, "Men of Galilee, why do you stand gazing up into heaven? This same Jesus, who was taken up from you into heaven, will so come in like manner as you saw Him go into heaven."
>
> *Acts 1:9–11* NKJV

One of the greatest promises we have received from the Lord as His children is related to His presence. He declares throughout the Bible, "I will be with you," "I will never forsake you or leave you," "My presence will go with you," "I will protect you," "I will provide for you," "I will come back for you," and "I will not leave you until I have done what I have promised you" (Isaiah 43:2; Hebrews 13:5; Exodus 33:14; Psalm 121:7–8; Philippians 4:19; Genesis 28:15).

Out of all of His promises, the one that changed the course of human history was fulfilled when the Lord came in the flesh to redeem us from our sins and transgressions. His coming was meant to restore the relationship and the fellowship we lost with God because of sin. God originally created Adam and Eve because He desired to have children who would fellowship with Him. He indeed fellowshiped with them in the Garden of Eden until the day sin and death separated them from God. God warned them to protect the fellowship with Him through obedience by saying, "You must not eat from the tree of the knowledge of good and evil, for when you eat from it you will certainly die" (Genesis 2:17). Adam and Eve lost the fellowship with God when the glory was removed, and they realized they were naked. Then sin and death entered the world.

God's children were separated from God, and they went into hiding out of fear and shame. God the Father came looking for them, but the detachment was complete. To restore fellowship again, humanity needed a Savior who would crush the head of the enemy. The enemy had deceived God's children, and only Jesus could restore the fellowship. So sin and death were revised by the coming of the Lord Jesus.

The Lord Jesus came as the second Adam, restoring fellowship by paying the price to reverse the curse of sin and death. This part of the restoration is our justification. We have been justified by the atoning work of Christ on the cross so that we can become the sons and daughters of the King of kings and the Lord of lords. Because of this restoration, we have been given the authority to be called the children of God and have full access to the Father through Christ Jesus, our high priest. By this, everything we were created for before the foundation of the earth has been restored.

The apostle Paul describes this amazing and great salvation.

> The judgment followed one sin and brought condemnation, but the gift followed many trespasses and brought justification. For if, by

the trespass of the one man, death reigned through that one man, how much more will those who receive God's abundant provision of grace and of the gift of righteousness reign in life through the one man, Jesus Christ!

Romans 5:16–17

Wow! No wonder that the writer of Hebrews referred to it as a great salvation that was foretold by the Lord and confirmed by the law and the prophets.

> This salvation, which was first announced by the Lord, was confirmed to us by those who heard him. God also testified to it by signs, wonders and various miracles, and gifts of the Holy Spirit distributed according to his will.
>
> Hebrews 2:3–4

Furthermore, this restoration has made us the righteousness of God to be His ambassadors on earth. "God made him who had no sin to be sin for us, so that in him we might become the righteousness of God" (2 Corinthians 5:21). This gave us back the right standing of being sons and daughters. Now, we can call God our "Abba Father" because of the spirit of adoption we received (see Romans 8:15).

Once we accept our sonship and reestablish our fellowship with the Father, Son, and Holy Spirit, we have no time to stand still and wonder. We need to redeem the time and the season by knowing and discerning His will and maximizing every opportunity by the Holy Spirit to live for His purpose. This was the reason why the question was asked, "Why do you stand here?" In other words, he was asking, "Do you know what He has done for you? Have you accepted your relationship with the Father through the Son? If so, why do you stand gazing up into heaven?"

The Lord Jesus was filled, led, empowered, and anointed by the Holy Spirit to overcome the temptations of the enemy, to preach (to bring) the Good News, to declare freedom for the prisoners of sin, to open blind eyes, and to set free the oppressed (see Luke 4:18). Finally, He gave His life for our salvation and was raised from death by the Holy Spirit for our sanctification.

Jesus gave His disciples the command to stay in Jerusalem until they were clothed with power from the Lord to be His witnesses (see Luke 24:49). After this final mandate, He blessed them and went back to His Father (see John 14:28–31). Instead of getting ready to get engaged in the Kingdom work, they remained, looking intently up to the sky. That was when two angels were sent to call them out. "Men of Galilee, why do you stand gazing up into heaven?" Essentially, the angels were asking, "What are you doing? Get a move on!" The reason He redeemed us, justified us, made us His children, sanctified us, made us holy, and gave us the Holy Spirit was for us to carry out His purpose on earth. We have been sent as the Father sent the Lord Jesus, who completed the work He received and glorified the Father.

The angels also reminded the disciples about their hope. "This same Jesus, who has been taken from you into heaven, will come back in the same way you have seen him go into heaven" (Acts 1:11). Jesus is coming back to complete our salvation by taking us into His presence. The phrases "this same Jesus" and "the same way" are very important. One of the greatest promises is, "Look, I am coming soon" (Revelation 22:12).

All these promises and more were waiting for the disciples, and now they are waiting for you and me. The disciples were standing still instead of redeeming the time. The Lord gives us grace for every assignment and for every season we go through. When we don't act within His timetable, not only do we miss an opportune time to honor Him in obedience, but we also waste the grace God provides for the season and the mandate.

The Lord Jesus Christ, who gave His life for you and has been preparing a place for you, is coming back to take you into glory. Are you watching and praying for His return as you do His will by living for Him? If the Lord sent His angel to you today to ask you a similar question, how would you answer that question about your life, family, ministry, business, and profession? You don't have any reason to remain looking for Him since He has already done everything for you to live for Him.

Are you using it or wasting it? This should be an everyday question for the children of God. Let's not waste another moment, because we have been crucified with Christ, and now we no longer live, but Christ lives in us (see Galatians 2:20). Hallelujah!

How would you answer the angel's question? Are you ready to be with Him?

Are you diligently watching and waiting for His return?

Are you living your life for Him and Him alone?

Have you been doing what the Lord has called you to do?

_____

_____

_____

THIRTY-ONE

Do You Love Me More Than These?

> When they had finished eating, Jesus said to Simon Peter, "Simon son of John, do you love me more than these?"
> *John 21:15*

The greatest call on a Christian's life is to ignite our passion for the Lord, to walk in truth, and to increase in love and compassion to fulfill His will. A person without passion is like a car without an engine. We can still admire a car even if the engine doesn't work, but it doesn't go anywhere unless we try to push it. Just as it is unthinkable to imagine reaching your destination by pushing a car without an engine, so is it to live a Christian life and be effective without deep, personal passion for God.

It's no wonder in the book of John that Jesus questioned His apostles about their level of love for Him. He didn't ask about their compassion in ministry, their capability to shoulder the weight of evangelism or building the early Church, or their desire for success. He wanted to know if they loved Him the most. The question the Lord asked Peter is applicable to all believers of all ages who desire to glorify the Lord through their love and devotion, as well as through their passion to obey His revealed will. Our love for Jesus is what prepares us for the assignment in our lives. We can't answer His question if we're not committed to live for Him.

Peter was the first person, after Christ's resurrection, who was faced with the question of love. "When they had finished eating, Jesus said to Simon Peter, 'Simon son of John, do you love me more than these?'" Jesus asked Peter three times, which must have seemed odd to Peter. He, however, answered the same question three times. The Lord responded by asking Peter to serve His people with compassion, telling him to feed, protect, and take care of them. Jesus then asked Peter again to follow Him. This request took Peter to the starting point of their relationship. Jesus knew that Peter was the person to ask this question of because of the revelation and wisdom in him.

Accepting the call of Jesus had brought Peter to the place of understanding or receiving a supernatural revelation about the Lord Jesus. This set him up with a strong foundation to love his Lord more than life itself and to eventually follow Him to the cross. His passion for the Lord and compassionate care for the people of God became part of Peter's life. That meant that the Lord Jesus had become the central aspect of his life and calling. From that day, Peter was not driven by a ministry, but by the love of the Lord Jesus. He retained his passion until the end. When he was killed for his faith, he was able to say, "Yes, I love you more than these."

Peter was used by the Lord to lead three thousand people to the Lord on the day the Church was born. This became the pattern, not only for the twelve apostles but for the fivefold leadership (apostles, prophets, evangelists, pastors, and teachers).

When He first encountered His disciples, Jesus didn't ask about their love for Him, but about their willingness to leave everything to follow Him. He simply said to them, "Follow Me." It was not a question; it was a command with all the authority of heaven.

They had free will to choose to obey or not. They accepted that call and followed Him. Peter reminded Jesus about that decision by saying, "We have left all we had to follow you!'" (Luke 18:28). Their willingness to follow Him meant He could prepare for them a step-by-step life plan as apostles of the Lamb of God.

Though Jesus began His relationship with the disciples with a "Follow Me," He later questioned their knowledge of Him. We all need to have a clear understanding of who the Lord is in order to be effective. Paul is a very good example of this because he accepted his calling by asking the right question. "Who are you, Lord?" (Acts 9:5). It is imperative that you have a clear understanding of the Lord and His nature in order to be effective in ministry and grounded in your walk with Him. The Lord Jesus asked His disciples once, "'But what about you?' he asked. 'Who do you say I am?'" (Matthew 16:15). "Follow Me" was the invitation, and "Who do you say I am?" was the revelation and declaration of who He is.

Peter received special revelation from the Father and professed who Jesus was by saying, "You are the Messiah, the Son of the living God" (Matthew 16:16). Jesus replied, "Blessed are you, Simon son of Jonah, for this was not revealed to you by flesh and blood, but by my Father in heaven" (Matthew 16:17). After this, the Lord started telling His disciples about His upcoming death and resurrection. They were now ready to hear it and ready to be prepared.

After His death and resurrection, Jesus revealed Himself to them again, and He went into greater detail regarding His plan and purpose for their lives. At this stage, they had been following Him for more than three years. They knew who He was. They testified to His resurrection. When He knew they were ready for their calling, He revealed to them the third dimension of their call. "As the Father has sent me, I am sending you" (John 20:21). In order to be sent, they had to receive the Holy Spirit. "And with that he breathed on them and said, 'Receive the Holy Spirit'" (John 20:22). The second thing they had to do was declare His love publicly.

The final question came before He commissioned and sent them out as apostles. "Do you truly love Me more than . . . ?" The qualifying factor is love. It was not only "Do you love Me?" but "Do you love Me more than these?" The "these" is personal. What you would place in that spot is going to be different from what I would. Loving God with all your heart, soul, and strength is the engine for your daily life and calling. For the people of God who love and serve others as themselves, loving God is not only the measurement of true success in life, but the only way to demonstrate the compassion of God. Let your passion for Him be evident to all because of your love.

Paul referred to this when he said,

> But whatever were gains to me I now consider loss for the sake of Christ. What is more, I consider everything a loss because of the surpassing worth of knowing Christ Jesus my Lord, for whose sake I have lost all things. I consider them garbage, that I may gain Christ.
>
> Philippians 3:7–8

Passion for God is an inner fire of love, holiness, worship, praise, and reverence that is inspired by the Holy Spirit, and it can't be quenched with external things. Song of Solomon referred to love when it said, "Many waters cannot quench love; rivers cannot sweep it away" (Song of Solomon 8:7).

Your passion for God draws you to Him, while your compassion for others enables you to serve and share burdens as you lead others into the fullness of God's purpose. The Lord Jesus, who became flesh and dwelt among men, paid the price for our salvation before ascending to the Father. In doing so, He gave people like you and me His Church. Yes, these men and women had a heavenly calling, but they were also following Him wholeheartedly, driven by their love and passion for Him.

He equips us to serve the Body of Christ with compassion "so that the body of Christ may be built up until we all reach unity in the faith and in the knowledge of the Son of God and become mature, attaining to the whole measure of the fullness of Christ" (Ephesians 4:12–13).

Accepting the call of God brings us to a place of receiving a supernatural revelation about the Lord. This provides us with a strong foundation from which we can love the Lord more than life itself. When Peter discovered this, he was not driven by a ministry but by the love of the Lord. He retained his passion until the end.

In our biblical journey, our love for God is the only true, unshakable foundation that lasts. Since love endures forever and it never fails, it is the greatest of all. Anyone who pleases God is not known by their skills but by their loving heart.

Do you love the Lord with all your heart, soul, and mind?

Can you truly say, "I love You more than these?"

If He said, "Follow Me!" could you leave everything to be obedient?

Having passion for Him is one thing, but do you also have compassion for others?

PROCESS THE QUESTIONS

To better integrate the material in this book, please respond to the following questions. You can adjust your answers every time you read through the material according to where God has you in your journey.

What three questions in the book had the biggest impact on you as you read through it this time? Write out your responses to these three questions.

Process the Questions

Which question is most urgent for you to act upon? Explain in writing why you feel such urgency.

What will you do to act upon that question this week?

Process the Questions

What will you do to act upon the other two questions within the next month?

Find a calendar and set dates to act upon all three questions.

Select a friend or mentor with whom you can discuss your plan of action. Encourage this person to hold you accountable for the actions you plan.

CONCLUSION

To honor God and be the generation that has an impact on our life and ministry is threefold:

- The first one is willingness to follow the Lord—to start right in a right place and on a right foundation with a right motive on a right path and focus.
- The second one is daily receiving the revelation of who He is to us so that we can walk the straight path He has set before us to reach our prophetic destiny.
- The third one is keeping our passion for Him by increasing the fire of our love for Him until the end.

When people base their value on the call of God, the knowledge of the Lord Jesus Christ, and the love of God, they will discover that those values have an impact beyond measure in their life.

ACKNOWLEDGMENTS

I would like to acknowledge first and foremost the Lord Jesus Christ, my King and Savior. My life would not be what it is if You had not chosen me to be Your son and counted me worthy of serving You. Your love, constant presence, and unshakable promises have made my life rich and rewarding. It has been an honor to serve You and the Body of Christ by Your grace, power, and Holy Spirit. This includes my speaking engagements and the many books You've had me write. I love You and am so grateful that You love me. Thank You for Your great plans and purpose in the remaining days. I look forward to all You have for me because I know Your glorious presence in my latter days will be greater than ever.

I would also like to acknowledge my wife, Genet, and my family for all the sacrifices you have made for me to follow God's plan for my life. Your support and love have helped me obey the calling of God to declare His glory among the nations. Words cannot express my gratitude to God for blessing me with such a wonderful family.

DR. ALEMU BEEFTU,

founder and president of Gospel of Glory, has a heart for training pastors, businessmen, and politicians with a goal of building national leadership infrastructures. Dr. Beeftu presently concentrates on transformational leaders of various ages in more than 55 countries who have the calling, giftings, and character to foster sustainable societal change for the Kingdom of God.

Dr. Beeftu earned a BA from Biola University and a master's and doctoral degree in curriculum design and community development from Michigan State University. More than forty years of practice in these and related fields has made Dr. Beeftu an accomplished and sought-after leadership speaker/trainer.

Dr. Beeftu's most recently authored books include *When He Opens the Heavens*, *Abiding in His Presence*, *Hosting His Presence*, *The King's Signet Ring*, *Rekindle the Altar Fire*, *Breakout for Breakthrough*, *Divine Pattern for the Fullness of His Glory*, *Restoration for Lasting Transformation*, *Igniting Leaders for Kingdom Impact*, *Wrestling for Your Prophetic Destiny*, *Put Your Heart Above Your Head*, *Restoring the Altar for Fresh Fire*, *The Leadership Journey*, *Spiritual Accountability*, *Leading for Kingdom Impact*, and *Determination to Make a Difference*.

Dr. Beeftu and his wife, Genet, make their home in Highland Village, Texas.

Connect with Dr. Beeftu:

GOG@GOGlory.org   @AlemuBeeftu

GOGlory.org   @GospelOfGlory

/Alemu.Beeftu.7